Getting Paid to Pay Attention

Why Your Business Suffers From A.D.D. and How to Fix It

Getting Paid to Pay Attention

Why Your Business Suffers From A.D.D.
and How to Fix It

Marilyn Strong

For additional information please visit:
www.GettingPaidToPayAttention.com

Library and Archives Canada Cataloguing in Publication

Strong, Marilyn A.
        Getting paid to pay attention : why your business suffers from A.D.D. and how to fix it / Marilyn Strong.

Includes bibliographical references.
Issued also in electronic format.
ISBN 978-0-921470-02-1

1. Success in business--Psychological aspects.
2. Attention-deficit-disordered adults.
3. Small business--Management.
4. Businesspeople--Psychology. I. Title.

HF5386.S77 2011   650.1087'5   C2011-908269-1

Book Layout by: Rudy Milanovich & Keith Leon

This book, and the information contained in it, is designed to provide tools to help you in whatever way you choose. Any slights against people or organizations are unintentional. It is sold with the understanding that the author and publisher are not engaged in rendering professional advice. The author and publisher specifically disclaim any liability that is incurred from the use or application of the contents of this book. Readers should consult a licensed practitioner for specific health care applications.

Permission granted by the World Health Organization to use Adult Self-Report Scale-V1.1 (ASRS-V1.1). The World Health Organization (WHO) does not endorse any specific companies, products or services in the treatment of Adult Attention Deficit Hyperactivity Disorder (ADHD).

Dedication

To all the business owners with ADD/ADHD—always remember YOU are brilliant!

and

To Lois Margaret Strong (Armstrong) 1924–2010,
aka Mama,
who first recognized how to direct and reward the creativity and energy of a daughter with A.D.D.

✍

Acknowledgments

With deep and unending gratitude:

To Keith Leon, whose book *Bake Your Book, How to Finish Your Book Fast and Serve It Up Hot,* provided me with the template I needed to get my ideas out of my head and on the screen and ultimately, on paper. Your comments and help throughout the process are deeply appreciated.

To my editor, Heather Marsh, of Classic Editing, who has the patience of Job when it comes to working with a rookie author with A.D.D. Thank you from the bottom of my heart.

To Cathi Stevenson of BookCoverExpress.com for the fabulous cover design.

To my readers, Alan, Bill, Kathryn, Peter, Russ and Scott. Your comments have made this a better book. Thank you so much.

To the women who attended my Kelowna Women in Business presentation in February 2008. Thank you for being my test launch on the topic of Business A.D.D.

To my mentors whose advice over the years I have gratefully received.

To Harold Davies, who was my rock when I began my entrepreneurial journey. He never stopped encouraging me or asking me, "Why?" I miss him every day.

To my mastermind group, Alan, John, Jason, Joel, Karen, Marina, Nadia, Peter and Russ, whose support, encouragement and anti-procrastination stance helped me get through the book.

To my family and friends, whose unconditional love and support over the years is gratefully received and returned a hundred fold.

And to Scott Pembleton who is the wind beneath my wings. Come, let's fly together!

How to Contact the Author

Email: getpaid@GettingPaidToPayAttention.com

Twitter: @Marilyn_Strong

Facebook: Marilyn Strong Author

LinkedIn: Marilyn Strong

Website: www.GettingPaidToPayAttention.com

Here's What People Are Saying About
Getting Paid to Pay Attention:

"Marilyn Strong's honest, human approach to conquering common business challenges sets this book apart from the rest. No-nonsense business strategies have never been delivered in such a delightfully motivating way!"
—Edward "Ned" Hallowell, M.D.

"Marilyn's strategies for handling procrastination, distraction and hyper-focus are thoughtful, original and fun!"
—T. Harv Eker, author of #1 NY Times Bestseller *Secrets of the Millionaire Mind*

"Turn your perceived weaknesses into strengths. Brilliance is not something you conform to, it is who you are. Marilyn's book will give you the insight to how your mind works, so that you can have the ultimate success in your business."
—Blair Singer, best-selling author, *SalesDogs®, Little Voice Mastery™* and *ABCs of Business Teams that Win*

"What a quick and charming read! Invaluable, tried and true strategies for every entrepreneur struggling to balance all the aspects of business on a daily basis."
—Adele Alfano, Canada's Diamond Coach, motivational speaker and author

"It's hard to run a business in this economy, and that doubles when you factor in the challenges that ADHD presents. Marilyn teaches the skills necessary to help entrepreneurs balance all aspects of business and continue to build and grow to new heights."
—Dawn McCooey, M.A., author of best seller
Keeping Good Employees on Board

"I was a small business educator for over a decade. I watched countless numbers of people do just what Marilyn has described...dive into self-employment as a perceived "match" for their working style. For someone with ADD, charting their own path is magnetic...the possibilities are endless. By the time many sought help, they were tired of wandering, multitasking, and having little to show for all the effort they expended. Many were still looking for the best "tool" or "idea." But really, the best tool you have is yourself."
—Barbara Densmore,
Professional Celebrant, former small business trainer, program manager and designer

"Getting Paid to Pay Attention gives a refreshing perspective on important strategies and techniques for every entrepreneur who desires straightforward advice from an experienced business owner."
—Debbie Bayoff, Certified Financial Planner, Investment/Insurance Advisor Dundee Wealth

xii

"Whether you're challenged by ADD/ADHD or not, Strong's book is a must read if you want to propel yourself and your business to the next level."
—Joan Posivy, author, speaker, entrepreneur

"Marilyn's genuine voice makes Getting Paid to Pay Attention a must-read for every business owner struggling with focus, implementation and organization."
—Dr. Julian Mendes, chiropractor,
Posture First Chiropractic

"This book is a brilliant antidote for a common affliction. Marilyn's thoughtful strategies are a cure for productivity losses that can bleed away profits."
—Kathryn Moen, owner, Moen Consulting

"Getting Paid to Pay Attention is as insightful on a personal level as it is in the workplace. Finally, a book for adults with ADD/ADHD that addresses business in a complete, honest and meaningful way."
—Keith Leon, book mentor, speaker & author of best seller
Who Do You Think You Are?
Discover the Purpose of Your Life

"These 3 simple yet powerful strategies can help any self employed business owner become more successful."
—Kim Duke, founder www.salesdivas.com,
International Sales Expert for Women Entrepreneurs

"After more than a decade working with entrepreneurs, I have come to believe the most important credo of a successful entrepreneur should be "know thyself." By practicing Marilyn's strategies, business owners with ADD—and even those without— can only succeed!"
—Lara Veltkamp, President,
Watershed Marketing Group, Inc.

"Simple, easy to implement strategies for success. And those of us affected by and inflicted with ADD/ADHD characteristics need all the help we can get, especially if it is simple and easy to implement."
—Lorna Rasmussen, author,
The Absolute Best Way to Make Money

"I'll admit it... I have Business ADD and that means I'm always chasing the next big internet marketing system. Luckily Marilyn's easy step by step approach and creative solutions have helped me get back on track and focus on less, in order to make more."
—Peter Koning, President, Entra Marketing Ltd.

"I've struggled with staying focused in my business, which costs me both time and money. By implementing just one of Marilyn's powerful strategies, I've seen a bona fide 63% increase in my productivity. Getting Paid to Pay Attention is an important work which any entrepreneur can benefit from reading."
—Russ Banister, CEO, Cyrus Ventures

Table of Contents

Preface

My name is Marilyn Strong, and I'm a marketing and business strategist, trainer and entrepreneur; I *am* my business.

I'm a woman of many talents, and I wear many hats in both my business and personal life. I'm pretty good at wearing several of those hats simultaneously, but if one falls off or sags below my brow, the others are sure to fall.

Why?

I have ADD/ADHD[1].

---

[1] The term ADD/ADHD is used throughout the book to encompass both A.D.D. and A.D.H.D.

There, I said it out loud. I put it on paper. I admit it.

I've had ADD/ADHD all my life. Unfortunately, schools in the 1960s didn't have the comprehensive tests they have today and no one—myself and the teachers included—knew why I procrastinated, was easily distracted and impulsive, had a low frustration tolerance or was chronically bored.

I can remember in 2nd grade we had to stand and read part of a book out loud. Starting with the student in the front left corner of the room and going row by row, we were supposed to follow the person ahead of us and read the next sentence.

Sitting in the last row, three seats from the end, I knew it was going to be a long time before the teacher got to me. Instead of listening and following along, which bored me to tears and frustrated me when the other students couldn't pronounce some of the words, I zoomed through the book, skipping things that weren't interesting. By the time I heard Miss Stull call my name, I was on page 12.

I had no idea where the others were in the book. I stood up and started reading from page 12. After five or six words, it was obvious I was on the wrong page. I was immediately chastised for not paying attention. Hearing the giggles of my classmates made my face turn red even through my freckles. I slunk down into my desk while the student behind me stood up and read the correct paragraph.

Not knowing where the rest of the class was in the book, I continued reading. Suddenly, I was brought out of my "reading trance" when I heard Miss Stull say, "Marilyn Strong! Stop reading ahead and pay attention." I can remember my face again turning red as I cautiously looked up and saw 28 pairs of eyes staring at me.

It was the start of hearing many teachers say and write on my grade school report cards, "needs to apply herself more," and "needs to learn how to manage her time" and "if she paid attention and stopped looking out the window or daydreaming she could easily get As and Bs instead of Cs and Ds."

Sound familiar?

By the time I reached high school the only reason I went every day was because of sports. It was the only time I really felt successful in school. I lived for them. My teachers and parents used sports and my position on a team as the reward if I passed my courses. As a result, my goal was to get out of school with passing grades while playing on as many sports teams as I could.

My parents could see I was struggling with schoolwork. I could focus on the courses I liked and were interesting to me. For the courses I didn't like, the homework was a long, unhappy, stressful and painful process combining tears, "Woe is me!" moaning and a lot of self-talk berating myself for not getting the work done before midnight, the night before it was due.

Fortunately, my Mama figured out how to help me.

Oh, you want to know what she did without reading through to the end of the book?

Well, she figured out my super sensitive hearing—an ADD/ADHD characteristic that some of us have—was one of my biggest distractions. Rather than let me listen to music during homework time, like all my friends got to do, she insisted I sit in the quietest room in the house with my back to the door and looking away from the window towards the corner of the room. We agreed on what I was to accomplish: read a chapter, answer some math questions or write my report—nothing that would take more than 30 minutes or so. On the table in front of me she placed: the assignment, a pen, pencil and eraser. Nothing else. No one else could go in the room, and I wasn't to leave until I had done what we had agreed to. I was amazed at how many times it worked!

There were other strategies she helped me test, which you will find as you read through the book. Over the years I've refined the strategies and created even more that I use every day. I'm astonished at how effective they are.

With Mama's help, I made it through high school without repeating a grade and was very proud of my Cs and Ds in the courses I could have easily failed.

Naturally my marks weren't good enough to receive admission to university, so I set out to find a job. The move from high school to my first employment revealed a whole new world filled with even more obstacles.

In *Driven to Distraction*, which documents A.D.D. in adults, Dr. Edward Hallowell, founder of the Hallowell Centers in New York and Boston and nationally renowned expert on adult A.D.D., found that 60 percent of children with A.D.D. carry the condition into adulthood—and into the workplace.[1]

That's between six and ten million adults.

I've since discovered I'm one of the 60 percent.

After several jobs with only one lasting more than three years and several lasting several months, I discovered that working for others wasn't the best time of my life. I felt all alone. I had the classic ADD/ADHD symptoms:

- I was impulsive, going off on tangents instead of doing my work;
- I was rarely late, yet I often procrastinated;
- I had a low frustration tolerance with people who didn't "get" what I was saying; and

- In most instances, after a short period of time, I became bored with the job.

Out of desperation, my last resort was to start my own business. Now, it's over 20 years later, and I've learned a lot. By continuing to implement these strategies, my business is finally going strong!

In all my years as an entrepreneur, I've met numerous other entrepreneurs who have ADD/ADHD—it takes one to know one. While we're very good at what we do, we're not always good at all the other parts of running a business: the filing, invoicing, bookkeeping, computer systems or, perhaps selling—whatever isn't our particular specialty.

As an entrepreneur with ADD/ADHD you may:
- Have great talents and training
- Be incredibly inventive and creative
- Be among the best in your industry
- Love the work you do with and for your clients, customers or patients

You may also:
- Have difficulty getting motivated to do work once you've secured it
- Have trouble starting work that doesn't play to your strengths
- Have trouble forcing yourself to do the

clerical, seasonal or maintenance tasks associated with your business

- Have a history of starting work or business that you don't finish
- Find things like paperwork and clutter consuming your personal office space, sometimes to the point where you want to go out and get another desk, and then...
- When you do start working, you're easily distracted to switch to something fun or better suited to your training...

If this sounds like you, you're not alone.

You may have been diagnosed by professionals; however, if you recognize some of the characteristics and that leads you to believe you may have ADD/ADHD, go to the Resources section for the link to the World Health Organization's self-test.

You're also discovering that parts of your business may have taken on similar tendencies. I call this Business A.D.D. It most often occurs when you don't pay attention and—whether or not you have a sound or flawed business model—the important and integral parts of your business are neglected. This neglect, if left unchecked, could result in the demise of your business.

It can be easy to ignore and neglect parts of your business you don't enjoy doing; it happened to me, and I wish I had put an end to my Business A.D.D. when I first recognized it.

It's taken almost 20 years to create and solidify the strategies that make up the ABCs of ending Business A.D.D.

In short, they are:
- Activate Your Vision
- Build an Accountability Team
- Celebrate

The best part is, along the way, I discovered my strategies have helped other entrepreneurs on the path to business success.

So, what are we up against globally?

In an article by Susan Young, *ADHD Children Grown Up,* she reveals that adults with ADHD are three times more likely to be self-employed owners of small businesses than people without ADHD.[2]

Compounding that, economists and politicians talk about small businesses being the backbone of the economy. In

Canada, the Canadian Federation of Small Business[3] reported that in 2010, 41 percent of the total private sector workforce was made up of businesses with less than 20 employees. In 2011, US President Obama called small businesses, which create two of every three new jobs in America, "the backbone of our economy and the cornerstones of our communities."[4]

Yet when you look at the statistics, it's frightening. In North America, more than 60 percent of small businesses fail in the first five years of operation. That's only a 40 percent success rate—a failing grade by any standard.

Considering that adults with ADD/ADHD are three times more likely to start a small business, it's safe to assume that a good portion of businesses that fail are owned by small business owners with ADD/ADHD.

So, what can you do?

How can you become part of the 40 percent success rate?

Nearly every small business starts out as an entrepreneur with a dream. From operations, to finances, strategy, marketing, sales and technology, the entrepreneur has to understand all phases of his or her business *plus* perform his or her specialty.

Add to that three of the biggest ADD/ADHD characteristics that affect our work life: procrastination, distraction and hyper-focus, and it's no wonder the small business success rate is so low.

I wrote this book to share the hope I've found and given to many other entrepreneurs with ADD/ADHD. All you have to do is these three steps:

1. Identify and acknowledge the triggers for your ADD/ADHD in your work.
2. Read this book from beginning to end! Seriously.
3. Take action.
   a. Implement the ABCs of Strong Business Strategies: Activate your Business, Build an Accountability Team and Celebrate, to determine which strategies work best for your triggers.
   b. Use the Action Plan in the back of the book.
   c. Test one or two of the strategies. See how they fit, and then test some more. See the difference in how your business functions.

When you've done that, I'm sure you'll be hitting the palm of your hand against your forehead and saying, out loud, "Of course!"

Introduction

My focus for this book was supporting entrepreneurs with Attention Deficit Disorder. In researching the content and interviewing entrepreneurs with ADD/ADHD, I discovered most keep encountering critical problems in the daily handling of their business, triggered by their tendencies toward procrastination, distraction and hyper-focus, so key aspects of their businesses are neglected. This failure to pay attention can cost them their business, their livelihood and their dreams.

It's a costly failure.

So, this book is about getting paid to pay attention and how great that feels instead of:

- The queasy pit in your stomach which fills your chest and presses on your heart and lungs when you *procrastinate* and delay making a decision or starting an activity.
- Chasing and picking up every "shiny penny" or "shiny object" that comes along. That's *being distracted*, not getting your work done.
- Staring straight ahead, with your peripheral blinders on to block out lights and movement, because you are late for a deadline. That's called *hyper-focus* and it's a cause of *not* paying attention!

My mission is to ensure that entrepreneurs with ADD/ADHD have strategies to help them in their professional lives, so the characteristics of their ADD/ADHD don't conspire to ruin their businesses.

Don't wait 20 years to recognize your own Business A.D.D. Start now before your business loses customers and you lose your business, dream and financial future.

Chapter 1
What is Business Attention Deficit Disorder?

In the fall of 2007, I was asked to present a business topic before a group of women. I was looking for a topic that was business oriented, educational and different. I wanted something the audience would remember.

I knew if I presented about something that I had gone through, I would put a lot more energy into the presentation, and it would come from my heart.

After my own struggles with ADD/ADHD and being an entrepreneur, I decided to look up the topic of Business Attention Deficit Disorder (Business A.D.D.) because I believed it was possible for a business—*and* its owner—to have A.D.D.

I felt confident that my experiences would be shared by some of the attendees.

If nothing else, there would at least be polite laughter.

So, my research started on how Attention Deficit Disorder affected the businesses of entrepreneurs with ADD/ADHD.

Since my presentation to those women in February 2008, I've found intriguing information that urged me forward to seek more. As I mentioned in the introduction, most entrepreneurs fail to pay attention to critical activities in their business. I call this failure Business A.D.D.

Business A.D.D. is a relatively new idea. None of the definitions or examples I found really talked about how it relates to the solo business owners and entrepreneurs who have ADD/ADHD.

I've found definitions ranging from the "inability to direct the senses to heed signs and pay appropriate attention to proper practices, applications, systems, processes, products and services"[5] to "the evil twin of business focus."[6]

Business A.D.D. is more than being too busy to do what needs to be done. It's more than the inability to heed signs or pay attention to proper practices. It's more than not being able to focus.

None of these definitions or descriptions really gets to the heart of Business A.D.D. as I see it.

Business A.D.D. is a syndrome common among entrepreneurs with ADD/ADHD. It most often occurs when you don't pay attention and the important and integral parts of your business are neglected. This neglect, if left unchecked, could result in the demise of your business.

I've owned several businesses, including one or two failures. One of the businesses that failed was a small publication.

I was distracted by implementing a new design for the publication when I took ownership. I hyper-focused on getting more sales and ignored what the customers were telling me about the product. I avoided dealing with the financial reality that my business model was flawed. I finally made the decision to close the business.

> **"Business A.D.D. is a syndrome common among entrepreneurs with ADD/ADHD. It most often occurs when you don't pay attention and the important and integral parts of your business are neglected. This neglect, if left unchecked, could result in the demise of your business."**

33

In hindsight, the three common characteristics of people with ADD/ADHD—Procrastination, Distraction and Hyper-focusing—combined with being an entrepreneur, contributed to the neglect of an integral part of my business: the business model.

I've since learned from my mistakes.

Business A.D.D. is rampant in many corporations, but in particular, solo entrepreneurs have a special challenge with Business A.D.D. Whether we know it's a problem or are pretending not to know by not paying attention to it, Business A.D.D. is crippling the North American economy by preventing entrepreneurs from fully contributing to the economic stability of their communities.

Do You Have ADD/ADHD?

Now, if you have ADD/ADHD, it's almost a slam-dunk that your business has it, too.

Maybe you've been diagnosed, or perhaps you're not sure if you have ADD/ADHD, but you're beginning to suspect that you might.

According to Dave Giwerc, a coach in Slingerlands, NY who specializes in working with people who have A.D.D., generally, people with A.D.D. do not work well in typical business environments.[7]

For those of us with ADD/ADHD who work, or have worked, for employers who didn't understand us, our performance evaluations likely included these words:

- Impulsive—instead of "can do many projects at once"
- Easily distracted—instead of "always willing to help others"
- Easily bored—instead of "comfortable with change and chaos"
- Overcommitted—instead of "dedicated"
- Tends to procrastinate—instead of "very hard working," "workaholic"
- Interrupts people—instead of "thinks and moves ahead of the world"
- Can be unnecessarily and hurtfully blunt—instead of "never holds a grudge"

Look familiar?

On the positive side of things, there are also benefits to having ADD/ADHD that both employers and we can miss.

Pete Quily, a coach who works with Adults with A.D.D., shared these insights on his website[8]:

When You Have A.D.D.:

1. You are compassionate. You can empathize with others and see many different perspectives.
2. You have a rapid-fire mind. You can do things quickly that might take others an extended period of time.
3. You have a high energy level. Adrenaline is a fuel source.
4. You are highly creative and think outside the diamond. Who decided it was a box?
5. You are a quick learner *if* something interests you.
6. You are constantly scanning your environment, which means you notice more and can find more information and resources.
7. You are a visionary. You can foresee problems and opportunities before they arise.
8. You are great in a crisis. You can create order from chaos.
9. You are a risk taker. Your impulsivity shows a bias for action. You're not afraid to act.
10. You are entrepreneurial. You think big and dream big.
11. You are a master idea generator.

Beyond these two basic lists, there are a number of additional tests, including those used by medical professionals in a clinical setting, to determine if an adult has ADD/ADHD.

One is the Adult Self-Report Scale Screener (ASRS -V1.1) developed with the World Health Organization and the Workgroup on Adult ADHD. This test was created by psychiatrists and researchers from New York University Medical School and Harvard Medical School. A link[9] to this self-screening test is available in both the Resources and References section.

If you want to be evaluated by a medical professional, please contact your physician to schedule a diagnostic evaluation.

Does Your Business Have A.D.D.?

As I mentioned, entrepreneurs, if you have ADD/ADHD or think you do, it's logical that your business has it, too, because you've carried over your personal habits to your work.

Here's a non-scientific, self-diagnosis test to determine if your business has A.D.D. To how many of these questions do you answer "True"?

Self-Test: Does My Business Have A.D.D.?

1. I prioritize the parts of my business that I enjoy, and often ignore the parts of my business I don't enjoy.

2. My workspace could use a thorough cleaning and organizing; however, it's not a priority.

3. "Close enough is good enough" when it comes to completing parts of my business I don't enjoy.

4. Some days I feel so overwhelmed at the follow-up I have to do that I wonder why I decided to go into business.

5. I'd like to save my mundane and boring paperwork for a rainy day in the Antarctic.

6. I spend a considerable amount of time doing work that isn't my strength.

7. There are days when I can't do the work I'm passionate about because I just can't seem to get started.

8. When I'm working on a project or task I'm passionate about, the rest of my business goes on hold until I'm done.

9. I'm dismayed at the distractions that continue to surround me and my work space, even after I've put significant effort into minimizing them.

10. Some days I wish I had employees so I could delegate the work I don't like and don't have time to do.

If you answered True to five or more questions, chances are your business has some level of Business A.D.D.

Now What?

So, now you've discovered you may have ADD/ADHD, and you've discovered that your business may have Business A.D.D. What's next?

Hang in there! Help is on the way. Let's look at the causes and symptoms of Business A.D.D. so you can decide which strategies work best for you.

In chapter 1, I mentioned three very serious causes of Business A.D.D.: Procrastination, Distraction and Hyper-focus, which contribute to the neglect of integral parts of your business.

In the next three chapters, I'll discuss each cause in detail. Then, starting in chapter 5, I'll provide strategies to help you move past Business A.D.D. and get on with being a successful entrepreneur.

How to Get the Best Results from This Book

In order to get the maximum results, I recommend you read the book in the order it's written. It won't take long, and you'll get the full benefit of understanding how the strategies help with different symptoms. Then you can dive into the areas and action steps which you feel will help you the most.

You'll likely notice as you read through the book, that I will encourage you to nod your head, or raise your hand, or do whatever you need to do to acknowledge your readings.

> **"I will encourage you to nod your head, or raise your hand or do whatever you need to do to acknowledge your readings."**

So, let's practice now. Go ahead. Nod your head a couple of times. Good, now you can stop. Now, raise your hand in the air. Good. Put it down. Now, you're ready!

Let's start with the first cause of Business A.D.D., Procrastination.

Chapter 2
Procrastination

Hands up if you have ever …

- Avoided a task or project because it was boring?
- Underestimated the time remaining on the task?
- Felt like throwing up or throwing your hands in the air and yelling, "ARGGGGHHHHH", because you didn't know where to start a task, so you put that task at the bottom of the pile?
- Put something off because you simply didn't "wanna" do it?

I see all those hands high in the air! Thank you for your honesty!

How quickly would those negative feelings become positive ones, if you could...

- Learn to identify the feelings and emotions that caused you to avoid a task, underestimate time and feel like quitting before you started?
- Change your behavior from negative to positive?
- Reward yourself through your work?

You *can* experience these positive feelings and emotions, make changes, move forward and much more. First, it's important to understand why these feelings occur. That will help you change your behavior and find rewards through your work!

What is Procrastination?

Procrastination is the action of delaying or postponing something that requires immediate attention.[10]

Dr. Piers Steel is one of the world's foremost researchers and speakers on the science of motivation and procrastination. He believes that people who procrastinate deliberately delay their actions, even when they expect they'll be worse off for the delay.[11]

For some, procrastinating behavior is a way of coping with feelings and physical symptoms that accompany depression, often caused by panic.[12] For others, procrastination is a mechanism to cope with anxiety related to the start or finish of a task or decision,[13] or it results from a fear of success or failure. Still, others justify it by saying they don't have time for the activity they are avoiding.[14]

The fact is, solving the time problem alone will not stop the behavior pattern of procrastination. (I can hear a sigh of relief from entrepreneurs who have tried a multitude of unsuccessful time management strategies!)

Why Does Procrastination Occur?

While issues surrounding procrastination are often emotional, there is also a biological explanation that encourages and even triggers procrastination.

Is It All in Your Head?

We'll need to delve into some simple neurobiology to find the triggers. Neurobiology is the study of our nervous system and how the organization of these cells helps us process information and mediate our behavior.

According to the principles of neurobiology, long-term *intentions* are made in the pre-frontal cortex of the brain. The pre-frontal cortex is also responsible for choosing between good and bad or right and wrong, predicting future events and suppressing emotions.

It is here that you create intentions to do things such as finish a report, make a sales call, create a new logo or practice a new skill, because you know the actions can lead to a good result.

Unfortunately, these good intentions can be superseded by impulses generated in the limbic system—the part of your brain responsible for your emotions—which is particularly sensitive to "concrete stimuli indicative of immediate gratification."[15]

So, while you intend to finish the report, create the logo or make the sales call, if the sound of a telephone ringing or the smell of dinner cooking happens—something that might provide immediate gratification—your intention is lost and you become distracted.

Then you pay attention to the distraction rather than remaining focused on your intention. It takes a conscious effort and some *Strong Business Strategies* to beat your brain at its own game!

Strong Business Strategies are powerful plans, approaches and tactics to use in the different areas of your business that will bring you closer to your vision and dreams of business success. You'll find these strategies in chapters 6, 7, and 8.

Now that you understand the neurobiology basics, Dr. Joseph Ferrari, one of the world's leading experts on procrastination,[16] has identified three types of procrastinators which can easily describe entrepreneurs.

As you read through this, see if you recognize yourself. In different situations you could be a different type of procrastinator!

Three Types of Procrastinators:

1. Thrill Seekers

Who are you? You speed through tasks to meet deadlines with moments to spare. You love this euphoric rush! You procrastinate to the last minute, get the work accomplished and enjoy the thrill of meeting the deadline by only a few moments.

Come on! Nod your head or put your hand in the air!

What stops you? You have trouble getting started and get bored easily. If the task is boring, monotonous or involves too much hard work, it stands a very good chance of getting postponed.

What motivates you? You like feeling the adrenaline rushing through your body, pumping up your heart rate and delivering energy to every nerve and muscle. You may also like the feeling of being on top of the world, of being in charge or even the feeling of fullness when you recognize you're content. You often find or generate these sensations either in your work or instead of work! You thrill seekers often love technology and try to figure out what it can do, so you can finish the job even faster.

2. Avoiders

Who are you? You Avoiders repeatedly postpone acts that would lead to success or more fulfilled lives.[17]

Have you ever noticed that jobs or tasks seem to get bigger and more unpleasant the longer you wait to do them? Yeah, me too.

What stops you? You fear success and failure—so you avoid both. That's often why you put off tasks that are unappealing. You avoid the butterflies in your stomach that creep up your windpipe. Your belief in yourself is governed by what others think of you. You would prefer other people think you lacked effort instead of ability.

What motivates you? You seem to have immunity to the *oughts* and *shoulds* in your lives. You know you should work on a project or task, but you'd rather do something else because the thought of working on the project or task makes you feel uncomfortable. It's the unknown of what will happen—success or failure—both of which you want to avoid.

3. Decisional Procrastinators

Who are you? You can't make a decision (actually you can make one decision—the decision to not make a decision!), or you postpone the decision especially when dealing with conflicts.

Hands up if you have all the information you need but still can't or won't make the decision for fear of being wrong or imperfect!

I see you! Thank you for your honesty.

What stops you? People with high decisional procrastination often display tendencies of perfectionism. You seek excessive amounts of information about the alternatives or options before making a decision. It's called *analysis paralysis,* and absolves you of any responsibility for the outcome of events.

You may underestimate the time left to complete the task or project. As the deadline approaches, you often shift into panic mode because there is so much left to do and not enough time. You can then become a Thrill Seeking Procrastinator.

What motivates you? The fear of being ridiculed if what you say or produce isn't exactly perfect and the necessity for perfection motivates the decisional procrastinator to take action. You focus on collecting as much data as you can. Then you proceed with caution, ensuring that everything is in the right order and correct.

◅

Final thoughts on Procrastination:

When you feel the adrenaline pumping through your veins, the butterflies going up your windpipe, or your face reddening when you've been ridiculed, or you don't know where to start, or just don't "wanna" do something, that's when you're most likely to procrastinate. Sometimes we ignore the important revenue-generating aspects. Other times we ignore the *ugly work*, meaning the work that is required to be done by *anyone other than our clients.*

For entrepreneurs with ADD/ADHD, if we believe that we don't know how to start a project, then all our thoughts become focused on the "not knowing." These thoughts can then lead to feelings of:

- Defeat: How can I not know? This is what I do!
- Paralysis: How will I ever finish when I can't get started? There's so much to do.

- Failure: I'll never get this done. I shouldn't
  have agreed to do this.
- Unworthiness: I'm not smart enough or good
  enough.

If this is how you feel, then your action can become inaction, also called Procrastination. These feelings weigh you down.

With the simple strategies you will find in chapter 7, you can turn your fears into triumphs and your shame into pride. You can turn your impatience into a sense of accomplishment.

When you learn to break through the procrastination causes and accomplish work that brings you a stronger sense of self, value and wealth, you will no longer be tempted to neglect the important and integral parts of your business.

Chapter 3
Distraction

Distractions are the bane of many entrepreneurs. Those with ADD/ADHD are particularly susceptible to distractions. As hard as you try to stay focused or on topic, almost any movement, sound, smell or touch can cause a distraction. This is often referred to as the Shiny Penny (or Shiny Object) Syndrome.

I like the term Shiny Penny Syndrome because it gives a simple visual to a complex problem. As I'm walking along a sidewalk, or in a parking lot, the sun reflects off errant pennies on the ground. They always catch my eye, so I'll stop and pick them up. I'll also stop for nickels, dimes and quarters, but the pennies seem to shine the most.

Shiny Penny Syndrome is where people—entrepreneurs, in this case—get distracted by too many ideas or have thoughts that go off in a million directions, making it difficult to get anything completed. Hundreds of thousands of hours of productive, billable time and dollars are lost when we're distracted by the shiny pennies in our path instead of focusing on our own work.

> Joe: How do you know if you have Shiny Penny Syndrome?
> Ashley: Hmmm, I don't know. Tell me.
> Joe: Oh, look—a bird!

In 2002, Tom Ranseen of Ranseen Marketing in Nashville, Tennessee said lack of focus is the Achilles heel of most businesses—large and small—and is the reason many end up not making it.[18] He hit the nail on the head when he wrote that succumbing to distractions is a hallmark symptom of Business A.D.D.

You're most susceptible to distractions and interruptions when you're doing work you don't like or feel you aren't good at. In fact, many people love the opportunity distractions provide because they can stop doing things they don't like to do anyway! Let's explore the types of distractions that affect our business and cause it to work less efficiently.

What is Distraction?

Distractions are interruptions that trigger a change in our focus which in turn stops us from moving ahead on our current path and sets us on another. If you give in to distractions you won't ever attain the strong, healthy and successful business you want.

Why can it be so hard to focus and pay attention to your vision? Why do you succumb to distractions?

> **"Why can it be so hard to focus and pay attention to your vision?"**

Why Does Distraction Occur?

Technology

In 2006, Pat Baldridge, President of the Women's Initiative Network,[19] talked about technology producing a malady that she called BADD (Business Attention Deficit Disorder). She said BADD simply makes us too busy to do what needs to be done. With all the technology we can access, the constant interruptions and distractions make us less productive.

A 2007 article in BusinessWeek[20] describes the term "environmentally induced attention deficit disorder," first introduced by psychiatrist Dr. Edward Hallowell. Dr. Hallowell says technology and activity overload can stimulate the environment to trigger A.D.D.

So, things like phones ringing, blinking lights on the printer or router and buzzing from your cell phone all contribute to you being distracted and neglecting important parts of your business to focus on the distraction.

Besides technological interruptions, our auditory and visual senses are bombarded by messages which distract us.

Many people with ADD/ADHD have acute hearing. All noises—fans and furnaces, mechanical clocks and so on— as well as visual distractions—such as clutter and dirty dishes we encounter in our home office are distractions that cause us to lose focus on our business, and we lose our business momentum because "we forget where we were in the task at hand nearly half the time after being distracted."[21]

If you and your business just can't seem to focus, because of all the technology distractions, turn to Action Step 7 for solutions.

Lack of Company Direction

A press release from February 2008, which introduces a book, *Big Ideas to Big Results: Remake and Recharge Your Company, Fast*, says corporate American business has been diagnosed with organizational A.D.D., with leaders steering rapidly from ditch to ditch, darting off at the next big idea that comes along.[22]

Entrepreneurs often fall victim to the same problem of not knowing how to steer their businesses in the right direction or even what the right direction should be. For those entrepreneurs with ADD/ADHD, the inability to focus on their visions is a symptom of Business A.D.D. This problem is further compounded when they're unsure how to describe their visions.

In one of his articles, Thom Finn, a business coach, talks about Entrepreneurial Attention Deficit Disorder.[23] He describes one of the symptoms of EADD as not being able to focus. If an entrepreneur can't focus or loses focus in the business, then the business suffers from Business A.D.D. A business without focus on the vision will never succeed.

Fear

Being afraid of failure or success—or both—can distract us from our vision and goals. As we clarify our vision, our insecurities creep in and one of two things can happen:

1) Your self-talk keeps you focused on what will happen *if you fail*. You discover that what you focused on becomes your reality and voilà! Failure.

2) Your self-talk prevents you from feeling in

control of your success, no matter how hard you work. Whether you don't know how to measure success, or you feel that, no matter how diligently you work, something outside of you controls—and often limits—your success.

> "Being afraid of failure or success—or both—can distract us from our vision and goals."

Maybe you're afraid because you don't know if you can live up to your past achievements, or fear that you don't have what you need to become successful and sustain it.

You might worry about what will happen to you, your relationships and your friends and family if you *are* successful? What if your loved ones don't like or love you any longer? What if they're jealous of your success? What would you do without them?

We'll continue with more about negative self-talk in the Internal Distractions section a little further on in this chapter.

For many people, fear of failing is easier to handle. Most are not afraid of failing because they have numerous personal and business examples of previous failures.

Learning about and expressing your fears—whether fear of success or fear of failure—will help you become more conscious about your behavior and which distractions prevent you from moving ahead. Being conscious and present will help you overcome the fears.

If fear often stops you, Action Step 3 is a good place to start.

You might still be afraid, but you will stop sabotaging yourself and be able to move forward.

Yes, it's scary. Yes, it's a change. Over the years you'll see that change is inevitable, so you might as well move with it, embrace and enjoy it. As one of my mentors says, "Bring it on!"

If you're ready to bring on the changes, turn to Action Step 10.

> **"If you let yourself become bored or distracted, be prepared for the unexpected avalanche of work that can result."**

Boredom

A second reason distractions occur is because you're bored or have to do boring work. Maybe you're working on a part of business you don't like or are tired of the repetitive nature of the work and don't want to pay attention to it.

There will always be parts of your business you won't like. You might prefer to work directly with people, either one-on-one or in large groups, so sitting at a desk doing repetitive paperwork where you're filling out countless identical forms by hand may be rather boring.

If you let yourself become bored or distracted, be prepared for the unexpected avalanche of work that can result.

Here's what happened when I let being bored distract me. Once I let several monthly envelopes from *Revenue "Ravenous" Canada* pile up on a corner of my desk. (Revenue Canada is the Canadian equivalent of the American IRS. I call them Ravenous Canada because they're always hungry for money.)

Filing papers is boring work for me, so I had accumulated more than 20 unopened envelopes. I assumed they were statements that showed I had paid online. Each time another envelope arrived it went on top of the pile.

That system worked until one September when I noticed my hefty income tax rebate hadn't shown up in my bank account. "Ah ha!" I thought. "Instead of putting it into my bank account, the government must have sent me the check! That means the refund is in one of those brown envelopes."

Sure enough, the second or third envelope from the top was information about my income tax rebate, which they were holding hostage for other paperwork they wanted me to file, and only after they received the new paperwork would they release my money.

Had I done the boring stuff on time—opening the envelopes, glancing at the statements and filing them—I would have discovered early that my personal rebate was being held hostage by business paperwork that needed further clarification.

The end result? I open every envelope the day it arrives, glance at the information, verify the account numbers and then deal with it immediately, even if it goes into the shredder. Yes, it's much easier to just stack the envelopes, but if I do what's hard, the rewards are always there.

If you want to stop letting the boring work build up, turn to Action Step 20.

You Don't Want To or There's No Short-Term Reward

How many times have you resisted doing an activity or task because you knew there wasn't a short-term reward in it for you? Sure, you knew the long-term rewards were there, but those rewards were so far away that by the time you got there you'd forgotten the reward!

Steven Pressfield, in *The War of Art*,[24] states that resistance is a negative force that stops us from doing anything "that rejects immediate gratification in favor of long-term growth, health or integrity." In other words, resistance is what prevents us from moving to our higher and more profitable selves. We're just being stubborn.

Remember the neurobiology section and the immediate gratification that the limbic system is looking for? Well, when you resist doing something in your business for which you don't receive immediate gratification, you're neglecting important parts of your business. That neglect could lead to the demise of your business.

Instead of blaming your stubbornness on your limbic system, which doesn't solve the problem, turn to Action Steps 20 – 23 for more solutions.

Inadequacy

Entrepreneurs are often not experts in the daily operations of a business. At times you will feel you don't perform in these parts of the business as well as other areas of your expertise.

For many of us with ADD/ADHD, the perfectionist inside us sets unrealistic standards that we know we'll never reach. If we don't think or feel we'll do a good job, we feel we shouldn't begin the job at all and search for distractions to prove ourselves right. Then, when the crunch sets in we do a poor job, and that poor job reinforces our feelings of inadequacy. How mixed up is that?

To find ways to get around this feeling of inadequacy, turn to Action Steps 14 – 19.

Stop Doing the Wrong Thing

You need to know your strengths and areas of expertise to generate money for your business. Then, if you find yourself seeking distractions while you're doing an activity that doesn't feature your skills, you'll know it's the "wrong thing" for you to invest your time in.

Although you might hesitate to contract out work you don't enjoy or aren't good at, the time you save can be invested in work you enjoy and areas where you excel.

> **"You need to know your strengths and areas of expertise to generate money for your business."**

Over the years I've taught many workshops and seminars about business and marketing to entrepreneurs. Whenever I taught a business start-up program, inevitably there was one participant who was determined to do everything—ordering, sales, fulfillment, paying bills, website development, and attending networking meetings. I knew if I found this type of problem in my seminar, this was a problem people often faced.

I cringe when I hear the entrepreneur *insist* that personally handling all aspects of a business is the only way to make sure the job is done to his or her specifications. The problem is one person can't do it all.

Here's a perfect example.

It's hard for you to justify paying someone else to do fulfillment. But, at the end of a busy day, you're tired and don't want to spend the hour it takes to fulfill that day's four orders. So, instead of contracting out the fulfillment, the orders sit and you promise yourself you'll ship them tomorrow.

Tomorrow comes and there are another eight orders to process. By evening, you've been on the phone all day securing more inventory, handling complaints and talking to customers. At the end of the 2nd day, there are 12 orders to be shipped. Each order takes you 15 minutes to invoice, box, pack and ship, so you need three hours to get the products out the door. But, your networking group meeting is in two hours, so rather than tackle some of the orders, you decide that all of the orders will have to wait until "tomorrow." And on it goes.

This is an example of the entrepreneur doing the wrong thing—your expertise is not fulfillment—and procrastinating about doing it. By spending your valuable time doing some of the wrong things, the parts of your business you're good at will eventually be neglected and your business will suffer from the lack of consistency and organization as well as a lack of revenue!

Now that we know why distractions can occur, let's look at the types of distractions that keep you from focusing on your business.

Two Types of Distraction

In his book, *The Pomodoro Technique,*[25] a time management method, Francesco Cirello discusses the two key types of distractions: External and Internal.

1. External Distractions

Unpredictable and often unwanted, external distractions trigger one of the senses: visual, auditory, smell and kinesthetic, or body awareness, to take precedence over the others. These are often simple distractions you face every day and prevent you from paying attention.

Visual distractions can include:
- Pop-ups on the computer screen
- Flashing lights on any piece of technology
- People or pets in your peripheral view
- Office clutter

- Any type of unanticipated movement or motion

Auditory distractions can include:
- Low level background noises, such as computer fans, lights or mechanical clocks
- People talking or whispering nearby
- Any non-regular noises, like doors slamming, phones ringing or a car alarm outside

Smell, or olfactory, distractions can include:
- Scented candles or room fresheners
- Food cooking

Body, or kinesthetic, awareness distractions can include:
- Temperature fluctuations in your body or the room you're in
- Body functions
- Pets near you, seeking attention

2. Internal Distractions

Internal distractions are distractions of the mind. They can be the toughest to rein in, especially when you're doing things you don't like to do. This requires a bit more explanation.

Research done by Dr. Daniel Amen, a world renowned brain imaging specialist, shows you have approximately 60,000 thoughts a day.[26] In a normal 16.5 hour day of being awake, that's one thought per second, 60 thoughts per minute and 3,600 thoughts per hour going on in our heads. No wonder it's hard to focus.

> **"You have approximately 60,000 thoughts a day."**

In an article in Live Science, MIT researcher and neuroscientist, Earl K. Miller, reported that distractions turn on different parts of our brains and do so more quickly than the daily grind of paying attention.[27]

So, if you have 60 thoughts per minute, and you're trying to focus on one thought or idea, when a distracting thought comes up it's no wonder you can be easily distracted. If this pattern happens over time, significant parts of your business can be neglected and will suffer.

I created three categories to help explain how internal distractions affect your business:

1. Urgency or Emergency
When a sudden task pops up, deciding if it's an urgency or emergency can help you prioritize so the rest of

your day doesn't suffer if you're struggling to get back on track after you handle it.

An *urgency* is something important, perhaps even necessary, but can wait until later in the day or another day— even though you'd prefer to finish it immediately.

An *emergency* is a sudden crisis that requires action.

So, how do you tell the difference? If the activity is sudden, unexpected and is something only you can do, it's probably an emergency. If someone else can do it, or it can wait until later, it's an urgency. If your mind compels or insists that you treat every sudden, unexpected task like an emergency, you are being distracted and parts of your business are being neglected.

> **"An emergency is a sudden crisis that requires action."**

2. Multitasking

So, is multitasking possible?

Psychiatrist Dr. Edward Hallowell describes multitasking as a "mythical activity in which people believe they can perform two or more tasks simultaneously."[28] Yet entrepreneurs with ADD/ADHD claim they thrive on multitasking; it's almost second nature to them.

Multitasking can also become multi-mistake-making and multi-never-finishing. Other researchers have concluded that it is difficult and perhaps impossible to learn new information while engaged in multitasking. It's more like continuous partial attention,[29] where we just skim the information, pick out the details we want and move on. We're paying attention, but only partly.

> **"Multitasking can also become multi-mistake-making and multi-never-finishing."**

To multitask or pay partial attention, your brain has to stop working on one project, switch gears—and perhaps lobes—to focus on another task. In the meantime, every minute of every waking hour there are another 60 thoughts racing around in your head!

3. Self-talk

Some people call what happens next a "crow" that sits on our shoulders. Some call it the *devil/angel syndrome*, the *little liar*, *head trash* or *little voice*. I call it self-talk.

You know what I mean. Right now it's telling you, "What self-talk? I don't have self-talk." Yet when you least expect it, the voice in your head goes on to punish, diminish, criticize and occasionally reward you—often negatively, no matter what you do.

It's the voice in your head that tells you, "You'll never be successful," "Your pottery is ugly," "You suck at _____."

If you do manage to push through that negative self-talk, what happens? That negative voice only partly becomes positive. It says things like, "It sure took long enough," "You could have changed a couple of words and made it clearer," or "Pretty good— for someone who doesn't know what he's doing."

For a long time I couldn't remember an instance when my self-talk actually used *only* positive words. Even when I received my hood for my MBA, as I knelt down, my self-talk was telling me, "Why did you wait so long?" when all I wanted it to say was, "Way to go, Marilyn, I knew you could do it."

Self-talk, in my opinion, is the biggest barrier to an entrepreneur's success. To counteract the negative self-talk, you need strategies to positively reward yourself every time you take a step towards accomplishing a task or project; and every time you pay attention to all the parts of your business.

Chapter 8, on Celebration, provides some great strategies to combat negative self-talk.

Now that we know there are external and internal disruptions that distract us and take us away from the important work in our business, the last section is on Hyper-focus and how it contributes to Business A.D.D.

Chapter 4
Hyper-focus

Hyper-focus is the final symptom of Business A.D.D.

What is Hyper-focus?

To hyper-focus means you focus and concentrate so intently on a task that you lose track of time and ignore everything else—and stop paying attention to the other parts of your business.

Entrepreneurs with A.D.D. can pay attention and, at times, hyper-focus with super intense levels of concentration.[30]

In some instances, this is a good thing. A lot of thrill seeking procrastinators get through their tasks by hyper-focusing—it's what gives them stamina. For entrepreneurs who are easily distracted, hyper-focusing can help them avoid distractions.

David Neeleman, the founder and CEO of JetBlue Airways, credits his creativity and out-of-the-box thinking to his ADHD. "One of the weird things… is, if you have something you are really, really passionate about, then you are really, really good about focusing on that thing. It's kind of bizarre that you can't pay the bills and do mundane tasks, but you can do your hyper-focus area."[31]

Neeleman has clarified the problem with hyper-focus, and explains why it is a symptom of Business A.D.D.: it's almost impossible to hyper-focus on a task or project that doesn't hold your interest—the ugly work. The problem is while you're hyper-focusing, other important elements of the business are left unattended. Talk about a Catch 22!

Why Does Hyper-focus Occur?

Hyper-focus in business occurs for two reasons:

1. You realize a deadline is looming and the time available to complete the project or task appears to be just enough. So, hyper-focus will help you get through Procrastination—which caused the need for hyper-focus—and get to the deadline.

Hands up thrill seekers who hyper-focus to get the task or project done on time! Me too!

2. You get totally absorbed in what you are doing even without a looming deadline. Say, for example, when you're researching something of interest, on YouTube. You can spend hours looking for the information. You have no immediate deadline to use or need the information—you just want to know more about a topic—and suddenly an entire afternoon is gone. Once again you've neglected an important part of your business and it suffers from Business A.D.D.

Typically, you would buckle in and work nonstop, ignoring family, friends and the rest of your business until the task or project was done.

When used properly, hyper-focus in combination with other strategies can be an effective way to get the ugly jobs done, as you'll see in the following chapters.

If you want positive results, you can't blame your brain for the way it operates; however, you can learn to work with the way your brain functions and overcome your need to procrastinate, find distractions and hyper-focus to avoid Business A.D.D.

Your new goal, as you seek solutions to daily business problems, is to follow steps that will overcome the limbic system's demand for constant instant gratification. Get that pre-frontal cortex—where you set the intention to start and complete tasks and projects—taking charge.

It's hard to be motivated to do something that doesn't have much value to you, or worse, is downright unpleasant.[32] This can become the "I Don't Wanna" Syndrome. Yet you know that unfinished jobs leave a lot of clutter in your mind and workspace, which in turn affects your productivity and leaves your business neglected and vulnerable.

> **"It's hard to be motivated to do something that doesn't have much value to you, or worse, is downright unpleasant."**
> **—Luke Muehlhauser**

The next chapters discuss The ABCs of Strong Business Strategies along with specific actions and action steps you can take to end Business A.D.D. and learn to pay attention to all parts of your business.

Chapter 5
The ABCs of Strong Business Strategies

So, now that we've explored some of the biggest problems, let's discuss specific solutions and action steps.

Getting Motivated

As we've discovered for entrepreneurs with ADD/ADHD, getting motivated to finish a task or project can be a challenge, especially if it's ugly work—remember, this is the work to maintain parts of your business you don't enjoy, not the work you get from clients that you don't "wanna" do.

During your normal work day, when you force yourself to do work you don't enjoy, you can often end

Getting Paid to Pay Attention

up in a negative state where you lack confidence, focus or direction. Your limbic system demands instant gratification. What if you can't figure out how to reward it? That's where self-discipline—the ability to motivate yourself to take action, despite being in a negative state of mind—comes into play.

Andrew Carnegie said, "People who are unable to motivate themselves must be content with mediocrity, no matter how impressive their other talents."[33]

Entrepreneurs aren't content with mediocrity, so let's get motivated!

What's the Problem?

How do you motivate yourself to do something you feel doesn't have much value, add much value to your business, or you just plain don't "wanna" do it?

Motivation Solutions for Three Types

- Thrill Seeker: Motivation is based on the time left to complete the work. When the work is an ugly job, there is little thrill to it. Hara Estroff Marano talks about the lie we tell ourselves: time pressure makes us more creative. He says, "Unfortunately, they do not turn out to be more creative; they only feel that way."[34] Finding

74

motivation to get through to the end can be tough. *Chapter 8: Celebrate has some great action steps to get you motivated!*

* Avoider: For all the folks who are easily distracted, look for ways to avoid doing the work or hyper-focus, there's help for you too! *The action steps and strategies in chapter 6 will help you activate your vision so you remain clear and focused on your business.*

* Decisional Procrastinator: Motivate yourself by investigating all the ways the work can be done, and then figure out which way is best. *Use some of the strategies in chapter 7: Building an Accountability Team to help you make those decisions.*

Your Three Key Strategies: The ABCs

There are three key strategies to help you fight Business A.D.D. I call them the ABCs because I believe they are the foundation for a strong business.

As you read through the ABCs, there are 23 Action Steps you can take to keep your business's foundation strong. These steps will help you fight through procrastination, avoid distraction and tame your hyper-focus tendencies.

Choose the steps that fit your situation. You may discover that combining some of the steps works well, or you may discover just one action step was all you needed to keep from neglecting parts of your business. Other days you'll want to work through and answer the questions in Action Step 10 until your task or project is accomplished.

There is no right or wrong way to move forward. Whatever works for you to overcome the neglected parts of your business and become successful is what's best.

Let's get started.

Chapter 6
Activate Your Vision in 11 Steps

Entrepreneurs, you need a vision of where you want your business to be in the future. To reach that vision you need goals. There are many books, videos and seminars on the subject of goal setting and why it's important. The difficulty for most people is in keeping a focus on the goals and activating—turning on—the vision they had when starting their business.

The Problem: I don't have a clear vision for my company *or* I don't remember my vision.

No wonder! It's pretty hard to activate your vision if you already have at least 60 other thoughts a minute running around in your head, can't remember what it is, or aren't sure if what you're doing is really part of your vision.

Some days you may forget your vision and goals as you get caught up in the day-to-day operations, distractions, work and urgencies. Or, perhaps so much effort was placed on getting the business started that clear goals weren't set. In either case, having clear goals and a consistent vision active in your mind makes it easy to get back on track.

When you don't keep your vision active in your mind, you end up with neglected parts of your business, which allows Business A.D.D. to settle in.

The Solution: Keep your long and short-term goals foremost in your mind and jump start—activate—your vision!

Here are my Action Steps for Activating Your Vision:

ACTION STEP 1: Create a Screensaver Vision Board
Often, people will have a vision board—a piece of poster board—with images of what they want in their personal lives. What they don't have is a vision board for their businesses.

On my business vision board, instead of putting it on poster board, I made a collage of images and used it on my computer as my screensaver slideshow. I used images of strong, successful businesses, images of what I do when I'm successful and images of the fun I can have. Some are my own photos, others are stock photos. My favorite image is a woman with her arms raised looking up at blue sky—a definite moment of celebration!

The screensaver slideshow only comes on when I'm not working on the computer for more than 10 minutes. So, when I return to the computer, the first thing I see are the images I have for my vision. Then my vision is activated and so am I!

I also added an image of my Mama in a red sweater and red Olympic mittens, holding the 2010 Olympic Torch to my computer desktop. Mama has the most beautiful, serene, calm smile on her face. It's hard to believe that a short four months after the photo was taken she passed away at the age of 86. When I look at her picture it reminds me that I can do anything I want to do if I want it badly enough. When my computer starts or I close down all my files, I see her. That motivates me to keep my vision active.

If you don't want your business vision appearing on your computer screen as wallpaper or as a slideshow, create a physical vision board:

- Compile a bunch of magazines with topics that interest you and cut out all the photos that are energizing.

- Look for words and sayings that encourage you.
- Go online, Google the images that inspire you and print them out.
- Paste everything onto a poster board.

How do you choose a location to post your collage? If it won't distract you, think about where your eyes focus when they're not focused on work. Do you look up and to the right or over to the left to see out the window? Do you like to look down on the desk? Wherever you like to look is where your vision board can be.

If you feel the vision board will distract you, then put it on the door or wherever else you will see it when you enter and leave the room.

Set your intention to make a vision board for yourself and your business and you are well on your way to activating that vision! Check out the Resources section for more information on Vision Boards.

ACTION STEP 2: Understand Your Values

When you created your vision for your business, either deliberately or intuitively, you based that vision on your values. Understanding your values and ensuring that they are compatible with your vision is an important step in activating your vision. If there is conflict between your vision and your values, you could procrastinate and allow distractions to prevent you from being successful.

For me, integrity is my number one value.

If your word is law and you do what you say you will do, integrity is one of your key values, too. Integrity generally means being honest and consistent. It's impossible to act with integrity while simultaneously procrastinating. If you procrastinate, people can't rely on you. If your customers can't rely on you, they'll go elsewhere, and your revenues will decrease.

> **"It's impossible to act with integrity while simultaneously procrastinating."**

Act with integrity and you will have a strong business.

So, what are your values and how do they help you activate your vision?

To help you along, I would recommend Greg Habstritt's Simple Wealth website[35] which has a free Success DNA Detector Quiz. (www.simplewealth.com/success-dna-detector.) After taking the test you'll receive an email with your five "success markers" or core values.

Once you understand your core values, you'll be able to see how those values are reflected in your business and your vision for your business.

For instance, if one of your core values is trust, then everything you do in business has to reflect a degree of trust: your trust in your clients and theirs in you. So, your vision has to state this.

When your core values are in synch with the vision for your business, you can keep your vision activated.

ACTION STEP 3: Create Some Thinking Time
I like thinking and challenging my brain, but I also like giving my very active brain a rest, because it likes challenging me, too!

Dr. Edward Hallowell, in an interview with Alorie Gilbert of CNET said, "You need to preserve time to stop and think to get the best of your brain. What your brain is best equipped to do is to think, analyze, dissect and create."[36]

You need to create thinking time. Thinking time is when you create a *void*; a place and time where you can clear your head of thoughts from the day and relax. That void helps you focus, calm your mind and activate your vision to see where you are. That void will provide the time to evaluate whether what you've done that day supports the fulfillment your vision. If you're off track, you can easily make adjustments so you're back on quickly.

> **"Your brain is best equipped to think, to analyze, to dissect and create."**
> **—Dr. Edward Hallowell**

Thrill Seekers need thinking time because you're always working under pressure and unrealistic deadlines. Your body and mind can only work under such stressful conditions for so long before stress causes problems in you and neglect in your business.

Avoiders, you need thinking time to encourage yourselves to take action.

Decisional Procrastinators already spend a lot of time thinking, but it goes in circles. Allowing too much time in some instances is why you suffer analysis paralysis.

Here are some suggestions to create a healthy void in your day: Be sure to check out the Little Picture Action Plan in the Resources section of the book for full details.

Creating the Void

      1. In the morning, during your Warm Up Ritual for your work day, focus, calm your mind and activate your vision.

2. During your Daily Work Ritual working on your tasks, be sure to include short 3 – 5 minute breaks and set aside time for your meals and snacks.

3. As you work through the day on those items, cross or tick off the accomplished ones. Yes, you can use a big thick red pen! As you cross them off, smile and tell yourself, out loud, "I'm awesome, I got _____ done!" *Be sure to check out Action Steps 20 – 23 to reward yourself!*

4. The Cool Down to your day is as important as the Warm Up. Yes, I know, there never seems to be an end to your day so here's a suggestion. Grab your Daily Action Plan for the day, take a few minutes to review your progress and congratulate yourself!

ACTION STEP 4: Keep a Daily Journal

Journaling is another powerful way to activate your vision. By writing out your thoughts, you gain clarity about your life and various situations. You also verify the progress you're making—which is REALLY important when you continue to multitask and don't know if you've made any progress. There are numerous books and articles on journaling. I've listed a few in the Resources section at the end of this book.

ACTION STEP 5: Brainstorm Using a Whiteboard

Another way to activate your vision is to think out loud and brainstorm with others or yourself using a whiteboard. Set aside a specific time each week or month to do some brainstorming using this method. It could be for an hour or half a day depending on what you want to accomplish.

Thrill Seekers love to brainstorm. They can fly through the ideas grabbing them from everywhere and anywhere. The more thoughts they record, the more thoughts come to the forefront, land on the whiteboard and they become excited.

Avoiders and Decisional Procrastinators can benefit from brainstorming. By putting their ideas on a board, they're visible to all. Avoiders can take pleasure in crossing out the To-Do items.

In brainstorming, Decisional Procrastinators can often visualize ideas on the whiteboard more clearly and understand how ideas that seemed unrelated before are actually linked together. This insight becomes the motivation to start and complete tasks.

Here are some simple How To's for brainstorming:

1. Start by writing your vision at the top of the whiteboard. Then, start recording your ideas. It doesn't matter in what order you write them. You could put them in a straight line, diagonal line or random on the board. Just get them down.

2. Some entrepreneurs use color coding for their ideas. Each pen can represent a different segment of the business. So, all the ideas related to, say, marketing, are recorded in purple; all the ideas related to finances are in black. Whatever works for you is the right way.

3. Look at the ideas and the vision and figure out where there is congruity. If you like to draw, draw lines that link items to your vision. The goal is that every strategy and idea that you're using in your business has to reflect your vision.

4. If your whiteboard has a built in camera that takes pictures of the content, make sure you take pictures and print before you start erasing items!

5. Sometimes just recording the ideas on the whiteboard is all it takes to activate your vision!

For more ideas and details on how to brainstorm, please check out the Resources section.

ACTION STEP 6: Talk Out Loud

Part of "thinking" time, doesn't have to be in your head. You can talk out loud to yourself. If you're thinking about something, saying it out loud often makes it easier for you to reason out an idea or answer a question. By the time you're finished talking, you may have several things you can record on paper and get to at a later date.

ACTION STEP 7: Meditation and Yoga—Mindfulness

For more than 30 years I had giggled and made snide remarks when people told me that they did yoga or meditation. I just couldn't understand how they benefitted by sitting in one position with their knees up their noses.

I've been humbled. In the last year I have discovered how practicing both yoga and meditation has helped me clear my mind of thousands of thoughts running through it so I can just *be*.

On the first day of my group meditation class, the first exercise was to close my eyes, breathe (doesn't that happen automatically?), count my thoughts in one minute and then let them go. "Go where?" I asked. "Just go," said the instructor. I decided *she* was going to be the receptacle for whatever thoughts I could let go.

That first time I tried it, I lost track of the number of thoughts I had. I mentioned earlier that Dr. Amen talks about people having 60,000 thoughts a day. I calculated that to be 60 thoughts a minute based on a 16.5 hour day. Well, I had way more than the 60 thoughts in one minute. And I still couldn't figure out how to send them to the instructor! But, I was willing to keep going until I could send her all those thoughts!

Meditation is a passive relaxation method. After a couple of meditation sessions, the number of thoughts started to decrease. There were time and space between the thoughts, and I could focus on my breathing. At the end of the class, my mind was clear. I could start thinking about my business and vision, and new ideas would come forward.

Yoga, on the other hand, is an active relaxation. Yes, you do funny poses with funny names. You may find that learning to focus on your breath in meditation will give you a head start in focusing on your breath in yoga. By focusing on your breath, the thousands of thoughts going through your head—the deadlines, phone calls you have to make, conversations you were involved in that day and things that didn't get done—all seem to disappear. When you're finished, you feel refreshed. Feeling refreshed can give you a new perspective on your vision and business.

I like to attend a yoga class instead of practicing on my own. As a beginner, I'm still learning the postures, and it's nice to have the instructor help me with proper posture and body mechanics. I aim to attend at least three yoga classes a week at my gym and, with the variety of types of yoga, there's always something new and different to try.

> **"Feeling refreshed can give you a new perspective on your vision and business."**

There are times you might find yourself in your office, having one of *those days* where every one of your senses is over-stimulated. That's when you can practice meditation or even some yoga on your own. Find a quiet place where you can sit, close your eyes and breathe for a few minutes. Focus on your breath, and when you're done you'll notice how much easier it is to focus on the activities that will keep your vision active.

ACTION STEP 8: Kill the Caffeine

I believe that what you eat and drink should nourish your body, not challenge it. In my opinion, chemicals, food additives and many foods compromise our bodies rather than support them.

There are many studies, articles and anecdotes about chemicals, food additives and some foods, like coffee and sugar, which seem to trigger ADD/ADHD and almost as many studies that contradict them.

I've studied my own body and discovered how they affect me. These are results from my own personal trials.

The smell of fresh brewed coffee can send shivers up my back and create a momentary distraction as my mouth salivates, anticipating a strong, bold cup of the black brew.

However, over the years, so many people had commented on my increased "spinny" state when I drank coffee that I decided to do an experiment. I gave up coffee for two days and then started it again.

When I started back on coffee, even though I was only off it for two days I discovered that caffeine not only made my body movements more jumpy and fidgety, I also couldn't think as clearly as I did for the two days I was off it. The more coffee I drank—and I could drink 10 cups a day— the more fidgety, scattered, unfocused and agitated I became.

I started and stopped drinking coffee over a period of several months in the fall of 2009. It didn't matter how long I stopped for, when I started again, that agitated feeling kept coming back.

I actually didn't think I could stop drinking coffee for good, but on January 1, 2010, I began my New Year's Day brunch with a cup of no-caffeine, Chinese green tea, instead of my usual steaming hot, dark, French roast brew. And my world didn't fall apart. The two-day withdrawal headache was a killer and the smell *still* makes me salivate every time—but I survived.

By January 4, 2010, my head felt clearer, and I wasn't as distracted or unfocused. So, I decided to eliminate coffee from my diet. I don't consume soft drinks so giving them up—with all the associated caffeine—wasn't a problem. I'm not completely caffeine free—I like the occasional chai latté—but I know that when I have one, I can expect some of my A.D.D. symptoms to rear their ugly heads.

Without the high dose of caffeine, it's easier for me to focus, I'm less distracted and this gives me more time to think.

Although many reputable doctors have actually prescribed caffeine as a treatment for people with ADD/ADHD, as recently as 2009, my personal experience contradicted this expert advice.

How about you? Do you consume caffeinated drinks regularly? Have you noticed if caffeine has an impact on you? Could you give up your coffee, soft drinks and caffeinated teas for a week or two and see if you notice a change in how you feel and how much easier it is to pay attention and keep your vision activated?

ACTION STEP 9: Dealing with Simultaneous Deadlines

Yes, there are times when simultaneous deadlines occur with many tasks or projects. Other times you can't move ahead on a project until you receive the information or a response on a particular task from someone else. While you're waiting for others, do you start a second task only to be interrupted some time later by the information or response from the first task?

When you get the interruption, if it's an appropriate time for a break, take one. Then shift temporarily to a second task. When it's time for a break from the second task and the new information has arrived for the first task, return to the first task and keep moving forward.

When it's time for another break, or if you've completed the task, depending on the project priority at the time, you can decide to keep working on the first task or return to work on the second task until it is complete.

This way you can feel like you're multitasking without the distractions.

ACTION STEP 10: A Framework—The Big Picture

Developing a framework—an outline—for your day can help you build time into your schedule, stay on track and keep the distractions to a minimum. (Remember to schedule time for chasing shiny pennies and you won't feel like chasing them when you're supposed to be working!)

You might think frameworks are boring and there's no room for creativity. Guess what? That's your negative self-talk whispering in your ear. Decide that your negative self-talk isn't your boss—you are. Learn to acknowledge your self-talk, by saying things to yourself such as, "Thank you for sharing. Now, be quiet!" This will help you move forward with what you need to do, without sabotaging yourself.

There are two types of frameworks you need to develop. There's the Big Picture Framework for each day. Then there's the Little Picture Framework for your tasks and work within the work day.

Your Big Picture Framework

Within your daily framework, create some simple rituals that are easy to follow, and can be done almost on "auto pilot."

It took me several years to develop and hone my morning ritual, but I realized after using it inconsistently, that I needed to stick to it or the rest of my day would fall apart.

Whether it's a work day or a weekend, the ritual for my day always goes like this: I get up each day at the same time—within one hour. When I leave the bedroom, I'm dressed and ready for the day. I head to the kitchen to put on the kettle and make hot lemon water, or I open the fridge and take out the milk and chai tea mix, mix them together and heat them.

I can be bored easily so my morning drink is rarely the same two days in a row, but I always have something, and it must be hot. As my drink is heating, I whip into the office and hit send/receive on the computer to let my email download. Then, I head to the front door to grab the newspaper and place it on the dining room table.

Back to the kitchen for my hot drink, I make myself breakfast—always protein, a carbohydrate and sometimes some fruit. I take my hot drink and food to the dining room table and enjoy it while I read the newspaper. Then, I'm into the office and quickly scan my client emails to see if anything will change my daily action plan.

Then I prepare my 15 Minute Daily Action Plan, and create my Little Picture Framework. Then I start whatever work or tasks I planned to do that morning. It could be a meeting, client-focused paperwork, phone calls or I could have to leave for a meeting.

This consistent, predictable morning ritual gives a structure to my day. Since I work alone much of the time, if I don't do it, I feel lost. When I'm not sure what to do next, I start spinning. The rest of the day I feel like I'm floating in the ocean without a direction.

My evening routine is simpler, and varies, but I always stick to a pattern because it helps me anchor my activities.

At the end of the business day, it's time for a gym or yoga class or some other type of physical activity. After supper I'm either back in the office for a while, at a meeting or relaxing. Just before I go to bed I have 20 minutes of exercises to help with my posture, and then I know it's time for bed.

Both morning and evening rituals are pretty simple. I can do both without having to think too hard; I'm almost on auto pilot yet there are many opportunities for variety so I'm not bored.

If you're looking for ideas and ready to create your own Action Plan, chapter 10 is completely devoted to creating your Big Picture and Small Picture frameworks.

Your Little Picture Framework

Often the biggest problem isn't with the big picture framework, it's the little picture: the daily tasks. Approaching these daily tasks without a system can cause you to be distracted, procrastinate or hyper-focus and may cause chaos in your business.

In the Resources section, I have a detailed Little Picture Framework that I use to put some context around the work part of my day.

Set out what projects you want to work on, what tasks *have to* be done, look to make sure what you're doing is keeping your vision active, and then block out times in your e-calendar to work on the tasks and projects.

If you find you ignore e-calendar reminders, use a timer that's out of reach and work on the tasks you said you would work on, in the time frame you gave yourself. No single task takes more than 30 minutes, you get your short breaks and rewards and then you're back at it.

By practicing this ritual, you're conditioning yourself to work in set blocks of time and react to the alarm when it goes off.

When you're dealing with the ugly work, 30 minutes can be a LONGGGGGGG time. If you find that you need instant gratification, it might be easier to break your ugly work tasks into bite-sized sections that take 5 – 15 minutes each.

> **"By practicing this ritual you're conditioning yourself to work in set blocks of time"**

Tax Time

The toughest ugly work for many people is preparing tax paperwork for the fiscal year end.

If this is also true for you, here's what an adaptation of what the Pomodoro Technique[37] for time management would look like, using tax preparation as the goal.

In preparing the fiscal year end for your accountant, set your timer for 15 minutes. Gather what you need and when the timer goes off, set the timer for three minutes and take a three minute break. When your three minute timer goes off, set it for another 15 minutes, to gather more information, take a three minute break and so on.

What can you do on your three minute break?

You can:

- Check your unread emails
- Grab a glass of water or quick snack
- Walk around a bit
- Do anything that keeps your mind off what you were just doing.

Continue this 15 minute/three minute break routine until you have all the items your accountant needs, all placed in one folder.

It could take you an hour or longer to gather everything because you've broken things down into smaller time frames. However, if you told yourself you had to find all the material before you could take a break, it might either take you hours to find everything because you'd get distracted and go looking for the instant gratification instead of the materials, or you would procrastinate and not get the materials to your accountant on time.

For other types of ugly work, creating a consistent, predictable ritual for your day and tasks will help you:

- Deal with distractions that remove your focus.
- Schedule the ugly jobs that only you can do.
- Activate your vision by setting aside the time needed to complete those tasks and projects.

- Avoid hyper-focusing on your tasks or projects.

Bonus Tip: Make sure your daily ritual isn't too structured. If the time frames or steps are too strict, you might sabotage yourself because your need for instant gratification will take over.

ACTION STEP 11: Stop Doing the Wrong Thing

The activities that you're good at seem to be the "right thing" to do, i.e. they're the best way to spend your time.

The activities you aren't good at are the "wrong things" for you to do, i.e. they're *not* the best way to spend your time.

How do I know when I'm doing the wrong thing?

There are two ways you might be doing the wrong thing. The first happens when you personally need to produce the product your business sells. The second happens, when you take on work that isn't your specialty, because you need the money or think you can do the work quickly and it won't interfere with your currently scheduled work projects.

In the first instance, you personally produce the product you're selling. For example, you're an artist and need to focus on your art because it generates revenue. Taking time away from your artistic endeavors to manage other business operations, like email, managing the money you earned or writing an article for your website may be the wrong thing for you. You don't enjoy doing these time-consuming things, but they are important to your business.

In the case of money management, after you've gathered all your receipts, invoices, deposit slips and checks, it takes you 60 minutes to input the data. That's 60 minutes you're not using to produce the product your business sells.

To compound your stress, you might feel like you aren't making enough money to pay someone else to do work, and *you understand* how to do it. So, you'd prefer to do it yourself. The problem is not that you don't understand how to do the work, but rather that you aren't as skilled at these tasks. Remember, when you're doing the "wrong thing" it often takes you twice as long, or even longer, to complete the task than a person for whom that task is the right thing.

How can you stay on budget, eliminate the wrong things on your To-Do list and make sure they still get done? You can do this by outsourcing or bartering.

ACTION STEP 12—Part A: Outsource or Contract Out
Find a person or business whose right thing, or specialty, is your wrong thing.

Hire a Virtual Assistant

Many entrepreneurs use the services of a *virtual assistant,* often called a VA. This is an independent professional who provides administrative, technical or creative assistance to clients, generally from a home office, often from another city, state, province or country. If you're looking for a VA, the non-profit organization International Virtual Assistants Association's website, www.ivaa.org, has a directory of more than 600 VAs in 16 countries.

Find a Specialist

Other options include hiring a commission-based sales person if selling isn't your thing, or building relationships with other entrepreneurs or companies for specific tasks, such as creating or updating your website, fulfillment of daily product requests, doing the bookkeeping, fixing or sourcing new technology and so on.

Make sure that when you're selecting the person or company to whom you're outsourcing, you consider it like a job interview. You will want to know what they're all about, how they work and what they will won't, do for your business. In other words, how will they fit with the way you do business? You're interviewing a new member of your team, and he or she should be a good fit for you and your business.

Email, Tweet, post on Facebook, or connect on LinkedIn, and ask your personal business networking connections for recommendations.

Take your time, interview and follow up with references and recommendations. Google them and check them out using social media. Do you really want to outsource work to someone who is constantly posting to Facebook? (That is, unless you want them to handle your social media!)

Find someone for whom order and organization is a priority. If your Virtual Assistant or Specialist can stay organized, there's a good chance this will help you. You can mention your ADD/ADHD, but don't outsource to anyone who will allow you to use your ADD/ADHD as an excuse!

In my experience, outsourcing to someone who holds you accountable works best. Choose Virtual Assistants who won't listen to your whining about why you might not get stuff in on time. If you don't keep your commitment to the timelines, your VA can't—and won't—keep committing to yours. If your VA and other outsourcing contractors can fire *you* as a client, it's an incentive to stop procrastinating.

> **"Outsourcing to someone who holds you accountable works best."**

Your VA can do the things you don't like to do, and that leaves you time to work on the parts of the business that make money and keep your vision front and center to your work.

ACTION STEP 12—Part B: Bartering

Another creative idea if you're an artist or produce the products your business sells, and limited cash flow prevents you from outsourcing the wrong things, try bartering.

Bartering is one of the easiest ways for entrepreneurs, especially home-based entrepreneurs, to focus on what they do best and find another entrepreneur who can do the rest. It's outsourcing without a direct exchange of money. While someone else is doing your wrong work, you can focus on your product or service and keep your business—and vision—activated.

Bartering can be done on an individual, or "one-off," basis, or you may choose to join a bartering organization. Check out one of the barter trade groups like International Reciprocal Trade Association (www.irta.com) or National Association of Trade Exchanges (NATE) (www.nate.org). Learn how barter businesses operate and choose the best one for your needs.

∽

There is a second kind of wrong thing that will sabotage your business: taking a job or project that doesn't fit your skill set or interests. Have you taken on work that didn't quite fit your skill set, or wasn't really part of your vision, just to have money coming in?

Yeah, me, too.

And what happened?

When you take a job that doesn't fit, you're compromising your values. When you compromise your values, you compromise your vision and neglect important areas of your business.

> "When you take a job that doesn't fit, you're compromising your values."

Big mistake. While you're doing the wrong work—and likely procrastinating because you really don't want to do it, you don't have time to find or create the right work that will activate your vision, keep you focused and keep customers coming in the door.

Doing the wrong work can also aggravate your procrastination tendencies. There are times you may decide to take on a client's work because you need the cash coming in. That happens. You understand the reasons why you're taking the wrong job temporarily. Remember to look at your vision board frequently to stay focused on your values. Develop a framework to get the wrong job done quickly so you can get back to doing work that activates your vision instead of triggering your Business A.D.D.

ACTION STEP 13: Use Technology as a Tool

One of my colleagues just switched to the latest smart phone. Not because it was a new gadget she could play with and distract herself from her work—which it did during the initial set-up, but because it was a tool to make her more productive.

When was the last time you thought of the technologies in your office as your tools instead of toys?

A tool is used to accomplish a specific task. My dad had a dented, turquoise-green metal toolbox, the size of a fishing tackle box. Inside were a hammer; a flathead, Robertson and Phillips screwdriver; a metal retractable box cutter; some picture hanging wire and a pair of pliers.

When my siblings and I were younger, our toys served as diversions, distractions and were for fun instead of serious practical use. My dad, on the other hand, had serious tools for a non do-it-yourselfer. He used the tools carefully, and we were *not* allowed to play with them. We watched him and learned an important lesson.

See and use your technology as tools not toys. Technology serves specific and vital functions for you and your business. It keeps you focused on your vision.

Just like I didn't play with the box cutter or use the hammer to fit a piece of puzzle into place—although for some puzzle pieces I swore it was the ONLY way to get the piece to fit—I use my technology as a tool. When I see and use technology as a tool, I can keep my focus on my vision.

Summary:

Strong Business Strategy #1: *Activate your vision.*
- Create and use vision boards and screensavers
- Understand your values
- Create thinking time
- Keep a daily journal
- Brainstorm using a whiteboard
- Talk out loud
- Practice yoga and meditation
- Kill the caffeine
- Develop frameworks and rituals that work
- Focus on the right thing instead of the wrong thing to keep your vision on track
- Use technology as a tool, not a toy

Now you're on your way to activating your vision and ending Business A.D.D.

The next strategy is about Building an Accountability Team.

Chapter 7
Build an Accountability Team in 6 Steps

If you're a one-person business and you don't have a great support team, building an accountability team will help you keep your business on track. An accountability team is like a board of directors you personally select to help build your business. They're a group of people who want you to succeed and want to do what they can to help you. When you make a commitment and need to be accountable, they hold your feet to the fire.

Often your team consists of yourself, your significant other or spouse, family and friends, mastermind group members (see Step 12), and of course, on an unstructured basis, your clients, although the list doesn't have to stop there. Sometimes mentors and coaches are great team members, too.

Remember that you're accountable to each member of your team...and that begins with *you*.

ACTION STEP 14: Become Accountable to Yourself

The first person you're accountable to is yourself. It's important to know what your key values are, because they set the standards for how you will do business.

> **"The first person you're accountable to is yourself."**

One of my key values is integrity, as I mentioned in Action Step 2. I apply my integrity not only in the way I interact with others, but also with myself. For a long time I allowed my ADD/ADHD to be an excuse for my behavior. I'd blame my ADD/ADHD for my thrill-seeking rush to the finish line, chasing shiny pennies, and hyper-focusing. I'd use it as an excuse so I could either avoid work I didn't want to do, or succumb to distractions without having to be accountable for the work that didn't get done.

I've learned through some experiential personal development programs that keeping my values true to myself is the single most important thing I can do, because those values are reflected in my business.

When it comes to business, your personal values are reflected not only in your business but in how you do business.

In Action Step 11 I talked about doing the wrong thing—taking a job that doesn't fit your skill set or interests just to have the money come in—and how that compromises your values. Learning to be accountable to yourself will help you make those difficult decisions easier.

ACTION STEP 15: Create a Code of Conduct

One of the strategies to build your accountability team is to develop a code of conduct for your business.

This code sets a tone for all the work you do and the decisions you make. It exemplifies your core beliefs and helps you define when someone you work with is violating the code, so you can decide whether to continue or sever the relationship. Your code of conduct is the foundation upon which you should build your business.

Larger businesses have several different codes of conduct—one for their employees, one for shareholders and one for senior managers. These codes share some of the same values; however, there may be responsibilities that are included with some codes and not others.

There are military codes of conduct, sport teams have written and unwritten codes of conduct, referees and coaches have a code of conduct and most professions have a code of conduct as part of their ethics.

If businesses like Coca Cola, The Home Depot and Walt Disney, as well as the military and sports teams, have figured out how important codes of conduct are, it's time that solo entrepreneurs took notice, created their own codes of conduct and made them a priority.

Blair Singer, a sales communication specialist, calls the Code of Conduct a *Code of Honor*. His book, *The ABCs of Building a Business Team That Wins*[38] provides the outline of not only how to create great teams, but how to create your personal code.

After I first read Blair's book, I procrastinated for more than three years before I built my personal and business codes. One of the key concepts in his definition was that of personal accountability if you violated your code. I knew if I violated my own code, I would have to call myself on it and my negative self-talk would set in. So, I procrastinated. Every time I thought of creating the code, I quickly found something else to distract me. My self-talk told me that intellectually I knew what my Code of Conduct was, so it wasn't necessary to write it down. If I didn't write it down, well then I couldn't be held accountable if I violated it!

Finally I was tired of carrying the weight on my chest when I thought of the code. I sat down and used Blair's ideas to create a Code of Conduct for both myself and my business. I felt the strength in my words and a sense of accomplishment at committing to writing it after I had procrastinated for so long. I now honor my code because it represents who I am and what my business is. I've included a copy of my Code of Conduct in the Resources section.

Being accountable to yourself first is the key to building an accountability team. If people see that you are committed to your vision, values and business, they will want to help you. Seek mentors and supporters who have the same strong commitment to their own values and standards, and you will start building a powerful accountability team.

ACTION STEP 16: Join a Mastermind Group or Create Your Own

The concept of mastermind groups has been around since the 1930s. Napoleon Hill, author of *Think and Grow Rich*, first defined the mastermind as a "coordination of knowledge and effort, in a spirit of harmony, between two or more people, for the attainment of a definite purpose."

The concept was inspired by a wealthy US steel magnate, Andrew Carnegie. "Mr. Carnegie's Master Mind group consisted of a staff of approximately fifty men, with whom he surrounded himself, for the *definite purpose* of manufacturing and marketing steel. He attributed his entire fortune to the *power* he accumulated through this 'Master Mind.'" [39]

Almost 100 years later, groups of business people continue to gather for the defined purpose to create mastermind groups.

There are groups like Business Mastermind Teams (www.mastermind-group.com), a membership site whose mission is to support small business owners to build successful businesses. The site matches up entrepreneurs with a mastermind group and an accountability partner.

No matter if you set up your own group, join an existing group or become a member of an organization that supports masterminds, there are three things to consider before you join:

1. Confidentiality—All members of the group must agree to complete confidentiality regarding any discussions. Some groups insist on everyone signing a non-disclosure agreement which restricts you from talking about anyone else's business to anyone other than group members.

2. Reporting/Rewards/Reprimands—All mem-

bers of the group must agree on how to apply rewards and reprimands. How do you report to your accountability partners that you've done what you said you would? What are your rewards and the reprimands for not completing your tasks or assignments?

3. Structure—How is the group structured? Do you follow a predictable format during each meeting? Is it a free-for-all where the whole meeting is taken up with everyone providing "free advice"? Or, is it something in between? Whatever format works for you and your group is the right one.

My mastermind group is focused on helping everyone in the group. We alternate between free-for-all and a predictable format. We are all entrepreneurs with different expertise areas in Internet Marketing. On every second Friday afternoon we meet together for two hours.

Here we:
- Share our frustrations, successes and challenges.
- Constantly learn and are challenged by peers.
- Commit to accomplishing activities that will bring us closer to our vision.
- Are held accountable to the group.

If any one of us is working on a task or project, no matter how mundane, boring, ugly or how much we don't want to do it, we are required to provide deadlines and updates. The recorder—that would be me—takes notes and helps us stay on track.

In my experience, there was nothing so humiliating or humbling as the day I went to a mastermind meeting and told the group I didn't do what I said I would. I was terrified, felt sick to my stomach, and I didn't want to go. I did what was hard by going to the meeting, and when it was my turn I just blurted out, "I wasn't going to come today because I didn't do what I said I would. I'm feeling guilty and very uncomfortable. I chose to tell you in person, because the thought of avoiding the meeting made me feel even worse. I won't do it again."

A few members thanked me for being honest, and we moved on to someone else. I don't want to disappoint my mastermind group again. They have the power to ask me to leave, and I don't want them to use that power, because their advice, encouragement and support to my business has been so valuable!

Does your mastermind group hold you accountable?

> **"Does your mastermind group hold you accountable?"**

ACTION STEP 17: Find a Coach

Coaches hold you accountable for your deeds and actions and can be wonderful additions to your team. You can use coaches when you're stuck. Their listening skills and direct questions probing into the center of circumstances you're prone to avoid might be just what you need.

Coaches ask questions; they're not advice-givers or sharers of expertise. They focus on you and your outcomes, and ask open-ended questions to help you understand what you need.

Your relationship with a coach may last a few sessions, months or years, so selecting a good coach is as important as selecting the best medical professionals, because you and your business deserve the best!

I recommend you search for a coach who is trained and certified. There are numerous programs, academies and universities that offer coach training. There are coaches who specialize in working both with business owners and people who have ADD/ADHD. If you're thinking of paying someone to hold you accountable, be sure to find a coach who understands, but doesn't sympathize with your ADD/ADHD.

One of my accountability partners used a coach to help keep her motivated when she was going through a mess in her business. The coach helped her clarify and work through what to set as a priority and helped carve out some personal time. The coach held her to her goals and within four weeks all was accomplished!

If you've never had a coach, check out the Resources section at the back of the book. You'll find a list of questions to ask a coach when you're choosing one.

ACTION STEP 18: Find a Mentor

Mentors are people who have achieved what you want to achieve and are willing to give advice and help. Mentors don't charge for their time and make great accountability partners, because if you don't follow through, their time for you becomes less and less.

You can start small by asking entrepreneurs you know if they would be mentors and set up a program of regular contact. You can also check out www.peer.ca for an extensive list of mentoring programs in North America.

I've had several mentors through my business career, some of whom had no idea they were my mentor. I watched their actions, listened to their insights and saw how people around them responded. I saw their results. Even though we may not have met, to me they were just as valuable as mentors as those with whom I had regular or occasional meetings.

Please remember there's a big difference between a coach and a mentor. A coach is paid to help you; a mentor volunteers personal time to help you. It's always easier to find someone to pay than it is to find someone who will volunteer.

ACTION STEP 19: Enlist Family and Friends as Accountability Partners

Find family and friends who will agree to hold you accountable for your business decisions or lack thereof. That's a wonderful gift they can give you.

My Mama was like that. If I asked her to proofread a document and told her when I'd bring it around, she expected it at that time and on that day. I never wanted to disappoint her by not giving her the document on time.

I have a very Strong personality—pun intended. I know how hard it is for close friends and family to hold my feet to the fire—if they can hold me down long enough to grab my feet—especially when they don't understand my business. But knowing they are rooting for me to be successful is a great incentive.

If you don't have the unconditional love and support of family and friends, when they don't see your vision or you're constantly being criticized, you may feel like you're facing an uphill battle.

If you identify with that situation, here are three suggestions, courtesy of www.thefuturepreneur.com/?p=738, to get support from family and friends:

1. Act as a salesperson. You have to sell your family and friends on your business just as you would have to sell your customers. So, involve them. Ask for their feedback; be open to constructive criticism of your ideas.

2. Address their fears. If the fear is about money—for example, that your new startup as an entrepreneur won't produce enough income to pay the bills, talk to them about how the business will be supported until the money comes in. Share the news of your sales with them.

3. Get them involved. Sometimes all it takes is a request for help or support. Ask them to do the right things for your business that are the wrong things for you.

Summary:

Strong Business Strategy #2: *Build your account-ability team.*

Now you know who you can have on your account-ability team. You may come up with other people and other ideas. Great! Whatever works for you is what is best for you.

Building your accountability team means:
- Becoming accountable to yourself
- Creating a code of conduct for you and your business
- Joining or creating a mastermind group
- Finding a coach(s)
- Finding a mentor(s) and
- Enlisting the help of family and friends

Your team members are only effective if you use them. If you've gone to all the trouble to build the team, then take advantage of their expertise to help prevent parts of your business from being neglected and causing Business A.D.D.

Chapter 8
Celebrate in 4 Steps

When was the last time you watched the players on a sports team when they scored a goal? Professional or amateur, there is always some instant and physical recognition by their peers of their accomplishment. There is a ritual to every goal, every touchdown, every hit and every win.

Celebrating the small wins and the big ones creates positive energy for the team and builds momentum. That momentum builds in each player, fueled by adrenaline, and is transferred to the other team members when they congratulate each other. As more momentum is built, someone else is energized to capitalize on the momentum and score a goal.

Hockey is one of my favorite sports. (Alright, they're all my favorites!)

> **"Celebrating the small wins and the big ones creates positive energy for the team and builds momentum."**

During Game Three in the 2011 Stanley Cup finals between Vancouver and Boston, Boston was up 8 – 0 at home, and Vancouver scored with only a few minutes left in the final period. Even though they were down by seven goals, the Vancouver team celebrated.

Immediately, the goal scorer's gloves and hands went up in the air while his on-ice teammates skated toward him, plastered him to the boards and glass and surrounded him in a big group hug. Then, the goal scorer led all the on-ice players to the bench where the rest of the team were already standing and cheering. As the line that scored the goal skated past, the players on the bench gave the on-ice team the knuckle bump to congratulate them.

What a great way to get the energy up and to celebrate a goal!

Even though they didn't have the energy of the fans behind them, their own energy was terrific and they celebrated. Unfortunately, the game ended 8 – 1 for Boston, but Vancouver did have one thing to celebrate—they scored on the Boston goalie!

There are many similarities between business and sports, but one of the biggest is the concept of celebration—celebrating *all* the wins.

You may think that celebrating your goal—the completion of a project or task—is no big deal. After all, with your ADD/ADHD, there may be times when you feel lucky just to get it done! You might rarely celebrate the small victories at the milestones along the route because, well, you just don't think it's all that important.

It is vitally important, especially for entrepreneurs with ADD/ADHD to acknowledge their accomplishments, no matter how small or big. Too often we denigrate our accomplishments with negative self-talk. We tell ourselves we "should've" done something different, better, faster, prettier than what we did do. "Should" is a punitive word that brings down energy and keeps procrastination, distraction and hyper-focus alive in our businesses.

It's time to stop "shoulding" on ourselves and celebrate all our wins!

Each win keeps you away from procrastination and being distracted. Each win keeps you focused on your vision. Every time you celebrate your wins you are rewarding yourself for being accountable.

Here are some easy and fun ways to incorporate celebrations into all your wins.

ACTION STEP 20: Develop a Reward System

It was from T. Harv Eker, in a Millionaire Mind seminar, that I first heard the expression, "Do what's hard and life will be easy. Do what's easy and life will be hard."[40]

It might sound silly, but after you do what's hard first, the rest really is easy. Then, once you start to practice this idea, it isn't so silly; it starts to make sense. If you let your limbic system go after the instant gratification by doing what is easy, life becomes hard because once the *easy* is gone, only the *hard* is left.

> "Do what's hard and life will be easy.
> Do what's easy and life will be hard."
> — T. Harv Eker

But, how do you motivate yourself to do the "ugly work", the hard stuff—the stuff that doesn't give you immediate gratification? What's in it for you?

"I want it *now!*" is the mantra of many. It's no wonder that having to perform tasks or boring, unending projects can result in your neglecting parts of your business. If you can't see the immediate benefits, you might not have the energy to start or continue.

So what can you do? Create a reward strategy for you and your business!

Create two types of rewards and prizes for yourself:
- Immediate rewards: Instant gratification for moving from start to finish of a task or project.
- Delayed rewards: To celebrate the project's end.

Both types of rewards work to:
- Defeat the self-talk going on in your head.
- Contribute to your need for thrills.
- Stop you from succumbing to distractions.

ACTION STEP 21: Create Immediate Rewards: Payment for Paying Attention

Clients pay you for finishing their projects on time and budget. But there's still other work in your business—work you can't outsource. This is ugly work and only *you* can do it. So, ordinarily, you would devote the bare minimum of time, resources and attention to it.

Then, when consequences develop, your negative self-talk steps in to say, "Why didn't you pay attention to the deadline?" or "Why didn't you get it done earlier?" or "Why didn't you pay attention to the details?"

I used to go through this. I'd even respond to my self-talk by saying, "If only I could be *paid to pay attention,* I'd be happy and wealthy!"

And then it hit me.

My clients paid me for finishing their work, whether it was ugly or not. What if I could be paid to finish my own ugly work, too? That way I wouldn't be tempted to neglect important parts of my business.

So, here's what to do.

Create a reward system for paying attention to those ugly jobs. Set up a series of rewards and payments for *paying attention.* Figure out where along the route you will have completed some milestones. At that point, give yourself a reward. That reward will encourage you to continue moving forward with the ugly work, and soon you'll receive another reward. Keep going until you've met all your milestones, and then be sure to have a nice payment when you complete the ugly work.

Now, these can't be just any payments or rewards; they have to match both your effort *and* be appropriate for the situation. For example, a three day holiday for 60 minutes of focused work may be excessive; whereas spending a few minutes with your animals or going for a short walk might be more appropriate.

Imagine for a moment you're a marathon runner. You've trained for months for the race. The gun goes off and you're on your way. At the first reward station you're expecting electrolyte drinks. Instead, there's a full roast beef dinner waiting. Totally inappropriate for the work you did to get to that station.

What do you do? If you eat the dinner, you might never finish the race because of cramps and vomiting. Yet, if you don't eat and drink something, how will you have the energy to continue to the next station where the correct reward is waiting?

Having proper rewards that are placed strategically to motivate you toward your goal are critical to your success.

The benefits of creating a reward system at different milestones are that you're:
- Creating the plan to get the work done *and*
- Defeating the negative 'self-talk' while *simultaneously...*

- Satisfying your need for instant gratification.

That's a win-win-win!!!

In my experience, the reward works best when it's something you enjoy and don't always get enough time to do. If you sabotage yourself by creating poor rewards, you won't get satisfaction from them, so you won't build enough energy or ambition to continue.

What if the reward is more enticing than the work, or you're tempted to rush through the work to get the reward? For example, if going to the beach was supposed to be your reward for doing work, but a trip to the beach kept winning without the work being done?

Rely on your Values (Action Step 2) and Code of Conduct (Action Step 15). If the reward is a trip to the beach, then work comes first. As much as you would rather spend the day at the beach, your personal values and code of conduct won't let you.

How do you know what kind of rewards will work? Well, different types of procrastinators respond to different types of rewards. If you don't get the rewards set out correctly, you might as well, as my Mama would say, "Save your breath to cool your porridge."

1. **Thrill Seekers**—You're more motivated by immediate rewards—instant gratification—than delayed rewards. Make sure you set them close together.

2. **Avoiders**—Your first reward should follow a small action step. Just like in hockey, once the momentum starts, place more rewards and prizes at milestones along the route to maintain your interest in completing the work.

3. **Decisional Procrastinators**—Establish a small prize as a reward for making each decision.

❧

So, What Are the Short-Term Rewards?

The rewards work best if they're personalized for you and reflect the effort required to complete the task. Here are some ideas, but really, you're the one who knows what rewards will work best for you.

Short-Term Rewards

*   Play a favorite song

- Spend a few minutes playing with the dog, cat or family pet
- Look out your window and marvel at the view
- Go for a bike ride
- Watch a movie on YouTube
- Take a walk around the block
- Go out for a specialty drink
- Make a phone call to a friend
- Plan a trip to visit a friend in another city
- Go out dancing or dance in your office
- Create your own exciting reward

If your mind and limbic system constantly search for instant gratification, learn to feed your mind what it wants, celebrate and reward yourself with what I call prizes. Remember to set a timer when enjoying prizes in order to develop a great ritual for getting back to work when time is up.

My personal favorite prize is to play a favorite celebration type of song, and then I dance to it. My all time favorite is Kool and the Gang singing *Celebration,* although Irene Cara's *Flashdance (What a Feeling)* and Taio Cruz's *Dynamite* are tied for second!

> **"Use songs to celebrate yourself and your accomplishments!"**

Go to the Resources section for a list of my top celebration songs and keep checking on my website www. GettingPaidToPayAttention.com for song title updates.

You will feel the energy in your body as you sing out loud—and off key—and perform your "happy dance." In fact, you can even add words to the song that fit the task or project you just completed. Create a phrase like, "the paperwork's filed," or "clutter is gone" or "marketing plan's complete" and insert that phrase into the song when there isn't any other singing.

Singing the phrases like you really mean them will get the blood moving through your body, which in turn creates energy, which then makes you feel alive. And you'll be inspired to get back to work so you can earn another reward!

Use songs to celebrate yourself and your accomplishments! Use songs as a reward several times during a project. The energy builds momentum. You will be in the moment and ready to continue.

> **"Celebrating the little wins and big ones beats back the negative self-talk."**

Bonus Tip: If you're having difficulty getting started on some ugly work, begin your work by first listening and dancing to one of your celebration songs. Feel the blood flowing through your body and your heart rate increase.

Movement increases the capacity of the blood vessels to deliver oxygen, water and glucose to the brain: foods that improve the brain's performance. When the song is finished, you'll have the "up" feeling you need to start tackling that ugly work.

Celebrating the little wins and big ones also beats back the negative self-talk. It's pretty hard to hear your self-talk voice criticizing and complaining above the band and music!

When you reach those milestones, acknowledge the reward. Savor it. Enjoy it.

Quick Milestone Celebrations

- Throw your hands in the air and wave them.
- Pat yourself on the back.
- Email your accountability team and have them send an "atta boy" or "atta girl" congratulation to you.
- Print out those congratulations and keep them in a file called "Pat on the Back." Whenever you wonder if you'll ever get through a difficult project, grab the file and read some of the wonderful things people have said

about you. Feel the energy the words create and feed off of it to keep going.

- If you're looking for a quick prize, put your right arm straight up above your head. Take your left arm and bring it out to the side, palm up. Then bring your left hand up to meet your right hand, and bring your palms together with a "slap" sound. Congratulations! You've just given yourself a high five![41]

When you set your milestone rewards and start working on the task or project, sometimes just knowing the instant gratification of a reward is coming can tend to make you work an extra step or two, because you *know* you'll appreciate the reward. Funny enough, the ugly jobs seem to go faster, too!

By the way, remember to set up little rewards when you finish parts of a fun project you *like* doing, too!

ACTION STEP 22: Delayed Rewards: Cashing In on Paying Attention

Now that you have immediate gratification placed strategically to keep you rewarded and moving forward, make sure you have a juicy, fabulous goal at the end of your project.

The second set of rewards you can create is called "Pay Attention...and Cash In!" You guessed it. Money is involved this time.

How do you cash in? One way is to write yourself a huge, post-dated check, dated on the day that a project or ugly work is due, and post it above your computer monitor.

If you complete the project or the ugly work *on that day*, you can cash the check and do anything you want with the money. If you like cashing checks and having money to spend, this can be quite motivating!

However, if you miss the deadline, then you get no check and no money to spend.

Remember, you're paying yourself for paying attention to the ugly jobs. You *want* to cash the check so you *will* get the project or ugly job done. Make sure the check amount is large enough that you're motivated by it.

ACTION STEP 23: Create a Reward System When You Stray From Your Goals

So, you've picked up this book and found many of these strategies helpful. Good for you!

What if, after all your planning, desire to do better and effort to change, you *still* stray from your goals, because you procrastinated, hyper-focused or got distracted? How would you handle that?

Just because you strayed from your goal or vision doesn't mean you're a bad person or will never get the work completed. Show yourself some compassion and allow yourself to have an off day. Stop the self-talk before it starts.

These are the times when simple forgiveness is your reward. When you forgive yourself, you reduce the negative emotions associated with straying, and you can focus on the good emotions and rewards that will help you finish the task or project.

> **"These are the times when simple forgiveness is your reward."**

Here's a little forgiveness statement I've created. You're welcome to use or adapt it to meet your needs:

"My team is disappointed and so am I. However, spending time lamenting or punishing myself won't change this set of results. I'm disappointed I won't get the reward I had hoped for and planned on. I forgive myself for the poor results. I know I can and will do better. I know what I need to do to get back on track and look forward to the next steps and the next rewards!"

As soon as you forgive yourself you can feel positive energy returning, and you're back on track.

Summary:

Strong Business Strategy #3: *Celebrate!*

Now you have so many reasons and ways to celebrate, you're well on your way to paying attention to all aspects of your business.

Celebrating means:
- Developing a reward system
- Creating Immediate rewards: Payment for paying attention
- Creating Delayed rewards: Cashing in on paying attention
- Creating a reward system when you stray from your goals

You get immediate gratification when you've completed a small task and your limbic system is happy. You'll receive delayed rewards so you're training your pre-frontal cortex. You get paid by your clients anyway, and now you pay yourself for completing, or at least working on, the 'ugly jobs'. And, if you stray, there's a forgiveness reward that will help you get back on track.

Create a reward system you LOVE!

Chapter 9
The End of Business A.D.D.

When you let procrastination, distraction and hyper-focus take on a major role in your business work, these characteristics can stop you from paying attention to all parts of your businesses. The neglect, also known as Business A.D.D., sets in.

What can help end the neglect? Practice the ABCs of ending Business A.D.D.: Activate your Vision, Build your Accountability Team and Celebrate!

Do it every day.

Just like the sports teams though, you won't win every faceoff, every down or every game. There'll always be a loss or a tie. Forgive yourself and move forward.

As more wins come along, you'll build the confidence you need to pay attention and end Business A.D.D. once and for all.

And a last note about hyper-focus. Hyper-focusing for long periods of time isn't healthy. That adrenaline, lack of sleep and intense mental activity all focused on one task or project means you have no energy or time for the other parts of your business.

You know, there's a reason for coffee breaks in businesses and recesses in schools. As I mentioned before, movement increases the capacity of the blood vessels to deliver oxygen, water and glucose to the brain—the foods that improve the brain's performance.

Sometimes focusing on a problem or task too much or too hard can get in the way of solving it. Taking a quick break will help your subconscious absorb the information, and you'll come back to the task or project feeling refreshed and with a new outlook.

Think of getting up from your desk and going to the office or home kitchen for a glass of water or even a quick breath of fresh air as your recess.

When your brain is performing well, procrastination, distraction and hyper-focus just won't appear. And if they

don't appear and cause you to ne'
business, you're on your way to enu

Ready to start your three action pla,

As my gift to you for reading this far, plu
www.gettingpaidtopayattention.com/dl/Action_Planner_
Attention.pdf and obtain a complimentary Action Planner ,
you don't have to make your notes in this book!

Chapter 10
Action Plans to Get Paid for Paying Attention

Here are three ideas to get you started on your Action Plans to get paid for paying attention:

    I.   Big Picture Framework, which focuses on the overall structure or framework for your day.

    II. Little Picture Framework, which addresses your tasks within the day.

    III. 15 Minute Daily Action Plan, which helps you begin each day with purpose.

First, let's focus on your Big Picture Framework. The goal is to create one main framework for your day. As you answer the questions, use the next three to four months of your life as the basis for filling out this plan. Then, if your activities change when the next season rolls around, you can change your Big Picture if you need to.

Yes, you can put ranges of time for your activities! And please note, creating this is *not* a linear process. You can work both ends to the middle!

I The Big Picture Framework

The idea of a Big Picture Framework is to have a loose structure around your day so, if you get distracted, or an urgency or emergency comes up, you can look at the plan and quickly return to the appropriate ritual.

There are four rituals to the Big Picture Framework:
    A. Morning Ritual
    B. Evening Ritual
    C. Daily Work Ritual
    D. Personal/Family Time Ritual

I've given clear guidelines to plan your requirements for work-days. Make sure to plan your weekends, too.

A. *Big Picture: Morning Ritual*

Step 1: Determine Your Morning Time Needs
        •   Determine how much time you *usually need*

in the morning between the time you get up and the time you're ready to start your work.

- Be sure to include personal grooming time, breakfast, exercise (if you exercise in the morning), any other responsibilities you may have, including kids to school or school bus and any commute time.
- Don't push yourself so you're frazzled before the day starts.

Most people need between 60 and 180 minutes depending on other responsibilities. Fill in the blank: I need/want _____ minutes between waking and working.

Step 2: Determine Your Work Start Time

- Figure out a good time to start work each day. That means the time you sit down at the computer, stand at the easel, or greet your first client.
- If you commute to your office, it's the time you start work *in* your office, so make sure you have included your commute time in Step 1 above.
- Do your best to start work at the same time each day (or within 30 minutes).
- If you're a sales rep, travelling or meeting clients first thing in the morning, then your

work day starts when *you're* ready. This may
not be the same time as your client meeting.
For example, your day begins at 7:00 am but
your first client meeting is at 8:30 am. That's
OK. If you don't have a client meeting first
thing, start working on a project or task.

Fill in the blank: I need/want to start work at
_____ am/pm.

Step 3: Determine Your Getting Up Time

You'll need to get up early enough to finish everything
without feeling frazzled.

Subtract Step 1 from Step 2. Fill in the blanks:

To start work at _____ am/pm, I need to get up
at _____ each workday.

Relax, it will work out.

B. Big Picture: Evening Ritual

Step 4: Determine Your Sleep Duration Time

Determine how much sleep you generally need each
evening. Fill in the blank: I need _____ hours sleep
each night. (Yes, you can put a range, i.e. seven to eight hours.)

Step 5: Determine Your Lights Out Time

Be sure to include time for personal grooming, reading a book, kissing the kids goodnight, preparing lunches, setting out clothes for the next day, time with a loved one and so on.

Fill in the blank: I need _____ minutes in the evening between the time I'm ready to go to bed and lights out.

Step 6: Determine Your Bed Time

To determine your bed time, start with the time you need to get up (Step 3), and subtract your required sleep hours (Step 4) *and* your time to prepare for lights out (Step 5).

So, if you must be up at 6:00 am, and you require eight hours of sleep, plus one hour to prepare for lights out, you need to be in bed by 9:00 pm with lights out at 10:00 pm.

Fill in the blank: I need my bedtime to be: _____ am/pm. (Yes, you can have a 30 minute variation.)

Now you've finished your morning and evening rituals. The last two parts are your work day and your family/personal time.

C. *Big Picture: Work Day Ritual*

Remember this is the Big Picture, so all tasks and projects are listed in the Little Picture Framework which follows below.

Step 7: Record Your Work Day Starting Time

Record your work starting time here: _____ am/pm.

Step 8: Determine Your Work Day Finish Time

What time do you need to finish work every day? Fill in the blank: I need to finish work at _____ am/pm.

(Yes, I know ending work is a hard one. Entrepreneurs with ADD/ADHD seem to be working all the time. This time frame must be before supper, with a 30 minute deviation.)

Therefore, I start work at _____ am/pm and finish at _____ am/pm.

Now, you have rituals for your morning, bedtime and work completed. The last ritual is for your family/personal time.

D. Big Picture: Personal/Family Time Ritual

This is the time left between when you finish work and prepare for lights out. Dinner, time to walk the dog, help the kids with home-work, take them to sports or arts programs and so on. All of those activities belong here.

Step 9: Record that time here. My family and personal time is from _____ am/pm to _____ am/pm.

So, now you have a framework for your day. It's not set in stone. Yes, you can have variations by 30 or so minutes. And some days your work schedule might start extra early or end extra late. That's ok. Work around those changes. Stay calm.

The whole idea is a BIG picture. A framework for your day. A way to get paid for paying attention.

Here's what my Big Picture framework looks like:

Marilyn's Big Picture Framework
6:00 – 8:00 am Morning Ritual
8:00 – 4:00 pm Daily Work Ritual
4:00 – 10:30 pm Family/Personal Rituals
10:30 – 6:00 am Night Time Ritual and Sleep

Can these times be flexible? Absolutely. Lots of time I'm back at work during my family/personal time. Some nights I'm not in bed before 11:30 pm. I set an intention and make a commitment to start work at 8:00 am so, no matter what time I go to bed, I still get up at 6:00 am because I need two hours before I start work at 8:00 am.

My morning ritual sets up my day to be successful, so those two hours are very important. If I take less time during my morning ritual, I feel I'm losing control of my day. I have trouble focusing, paying attention and getting going.

∾

II. Little Picture Framework

The Little Picture Framework contains all the parts of your work day, from the time you start work until the time you quit work.

There are three rituals to the Little Picture Framework:
>   A. Warm Up
>   B. Daily Work
>   C. Cool Down

A. Warm Up Ritual

Step 1: Set aside 15 minutes at the beginning of each day to create your 15 Minute Daily Action Plan.

A copy of this action plan follows this section.

Step 2: Now you know your plan of attack and rewards for your Daily Work rituals, take 5 minutes and make a list of the day's projects.

One project is fine but please, no more than four different projects. Otherwise, your heart will start to flutter and those butterflies will start coming up your throat and you'll start to defeat yourself before you start.

Step 3: Open your e-calendar and start booking appointments *with yourself*.

As you schedule the project tasks, group the tasks together. Then, schedule them into blocks of time that make sense for you.

For instance, if you have three projects to work on today and you're working from 8:00 am to 1:00 pm , then you're taking lunch, and working again from 1:30 pm to 5:00 pm, you could spend three hours performing the nine tasks for one project in the morning and two hours performing 12 tasks for your second project. Then, after lunch, you could spend the afternoon working on just one project and 14 tasks.

Remember: Those blocks of time have to include short breaks and rewards. No single task can be more than 30 minutes in length. This is NOT a hyper-focus marathon!

Step 4: If you find pop-up appointment reminders distracting, set a timer to go off at the end of each task time.

If you want the timer as part of your computer, the Apple iTunes store sells an inexpensive Task Timer for Mac and PCs—The Anti-Procrastinator Timer—by Endangered Apps. *Check the Resources section at the end of the book for more information.*

For those who need a timer but tend to ignore it and continue working, try this trick: Set a timer or alarm across or out of the room—out of reach—to go off at a set time. No matter what you are doing, the sound will be so annoying you will have to stop, stand up and go turn it off.

Bonus Tip: You can do this with the alarm in your bedroom, too. When you have to get up to turn it off, it's more difficult to go back to bed and back to sleep.

Once the timer goes off, set it for the length of your break—generally two or three minutes. When the timer tells you that your break is over, repeat the pattern by setting the timer for your task time—generally 15 or 30 minutes

This process will take longer to read than it does to perform. Honest!

B. Daily Work Ritual

You've already identified your tasks, projects, breaks, activities and rewards. So, now it's time to do the work!

Good, you're finished. Now it's time for the Cool Down Ritual.

C. Cool Down Ritual

Step 1: Grab your Daily Action Plan for the day and take a few minutes to review your progress.

Step 2: Put away the papers or equipment you don't need, tidy up a bit.

Step 3: It's time for your final reward for your work day.

What will it be? A high five? A dance? A run? Some hugs with the kids? Be nice to yourself!

III. 15 Minute Daily Action Plan

An advantage to having a daily action plan is that you can prepare for challenges before you start your day, rather than letting them creep up and distract you, causing you to procrastinate or hyper-focus.

Here's a 15 Minute Daily Action Plan to fit in your morning ritual time *before* you start work. *Create an intention to practice using this plan every morning for a week.* Promise? Cross your heart? Good. At the end of the week, you'll notice your results.

There are Seven Steps to your 15 Minute Daily Action Plan:

1. Set your intention
2. Determine the hardest task or project
3. Determine the Action Steps you'll take
4. Figure out from where your distractions could come
5. Record the accountability partners you'll use
6. Finish preparations
7. GO!

Your 15 Minute Daily Action Plan:

Step 1: Set your intention to end Business A.D.D. (2 minutes.)

- Make a master list of positive statements about yourself, your abilities and your business. Review the list of Coach Quily's positives about ADD/ADHD (chapter 1).
- Choose two to five statements that best fit you today.
- Repeat today's affirmations out loud five times.

Step 2: Answer this question: What is the hardest task or project today? (7 minutes.)

- Quickly record your thoughts about the challenges associated with your hardest task.
- Record where your ADD/ADHD might sabotage you on the hardest task. Be honest— the sabotage is there—see if you can identify it ahead of time. Then be prepared when it strikes.

Step 3: Determine which of these Actions Steps you'll take when an ADD/ADHD characteristic you identified above rears its ugly head. (1 minute.)

1. Activate your vision

   Will you...

   > Review and commit to your values?
   >
   > Create some thinking time?
   >
   > Write in your journal?
   >
   > Brainstorm using a whiteboard?
   >
   > Talk out loud?
   >
   > Meditate or practice yoga?
   >
   > Kill the caffeine?
   >
   > Use technology as a tool?
   >
   > Outsource the wrong thing?

2. Build an accountability team

   How will you...

   > Become accountable to yourself?
   >
   > Honor your code of conduct?
   >
   > Ask for help from your mastermind group?
   >
   > Ask for help from a coach or mentor?
   >
   > Enlist help from family or friends?

3. How will you celebrate progress on the hardest task?

   What will you do to celebrate the completion?

   What is your reward system for...

   - Making progress (milestones) during your project (i.e.: for paying attention)?
   - Finishing your project on time (i.e.: for cashing in on paying attention)?
   - Straying from your goals?

Step 4: Decide ahead of time which distraction(s) you'll allow yourself to pay attention to today and for how long? (3 minutes.)

- Family?
- Friends?
- Cell phone?
- Email?
- Other?

Then, be ruthless about adhering to your list. (For example, if your best friend calls unexpectedly and wants to chat, either decide in advance that you won't pick up the phone until after 6:00 pm, or allow yourself to talk for 10 minutes. Set your timer for 10 minutes. Your friend will hear it and you can say, "Gotta go, talk to you soon." Hang up and then get right back to work.

Step 5: Record which accountability partner(s) will hold your feet to the fire today when it starts getting tough. (1 minute.)

- What will your partner do to hold you accountable?
- How will they accomplish that?

Step 6: Get your timer, your materials, your Little Picture Action Plan and your focus ready. (1 minute.)

Step 7: Go!

You might answer some questions faster than the time frame I've given, or you may need more time. That's fine. Whatever you do, make sure the benefits work!

Results

You've done this for a week. Remember? You promised!

Now it's time to look at your results. Nod your head or put your right hand in the air when:
- You noticed you did things differently and got better results.
- There were fewer distractions competing for your attention.
- You felt less need to hyper-focus.
- Your procrastination tendencies retreated.
- The neglected parts of your business received some attention now.
- You felt in control of your business instead of feeling your business controlling you.

Yes?

Congratulations!

It's time for your last celebration. Put (or keep) your right hand in the air, palm facing to the left. Put your left hand out to the side, palm up. Quickly bring your left hand up to your right hand and slap it.

You've given yourself a high five and you're on your way to Getting Paid to Pay Attention and Ending Business A.D.D.!

Resources

Adult Self Report Scale for ADHD
World Health Organization,
Adult Self-Report Scale-V1.1 (ASRS-V1.1)
www.gettingpaidtopayattention.com/adhd-test

Brainstorming
Baumgartner, Jeffrey Paul.
The Step by Step Guide to Brainstorming,
www.jpb.com/creative/brainstorming.php
BusinessBalls.com
www.businessballs.com/brainstorming.htm

Coaching
Questions to ask potential coaches:
Have you had any formal training?
If not, how long have you been a coach?
If yes, what is your training?
Are you a member of the International Coaches Federation?
How long have you been a member?
Do you belong to another recognized coaching organization?
How many clients have you had since you started?
What is your preferred way of working with clients—on the phone or in person?
Could you specify time frames, rates and how fees are paid?
Are there any past or present clients who would provide a referral?

Code of Conduct: Marilyn Strong

My family members are the most important people in my life. They come first.

I continually challenge myself to be and do better

I surround myself with people who challenge me to be better.

I will address an issue when it arises.

When I have a problem, I will stick with it until I can resolve it.

My word is my honor—I will do what I say without excuses.

I speak the truth.

I will never go to bed with anger or an outstanding issue.

I always maintain the highest ethical standards. If I am uncomfortable with something, I will stop and work through it until I no longer feel uncomfortable.

I will be honest with people and in my dealings with people.

I will look after my own health and stay within the guidelines to remain healthy.

I look for opportunities for personal growth.

My key values are integrity and honesty.

I do what's hard first and then do what's easy.

I count on my accountability team to "call me out" when I'm not living up to my code and support me until I'm back on track.

I rely on my integrity to "call" myself when I'm not living up to my code.

I practice and live by the words: "It's not my news to tell."

Code of Conduct:
The Strong Communication Group, Inc.

We add value to everything we do.

We will ensure that everyone we meet knows where our focus and value lies.

We will charge fees for the value we bring and be rewarded for that value.

We will always be fair with our customers and clients.

We will stay current with all our operations.

We will be open and upfront about any areas or issues we encounter.

We will admit mistakes when we make them.

De-Cluttering

National Association of Professional Organizers
www.napo.net
Professional Organizers in Canada
www.organizersincanada.com
International Association of Professional Organizers
www.organizingtheworld.com
Faithful Organizers
www.faithfulorganizers.com
International Association of Virtual Organizers
www.virtualorganizersconnect.com

Journaling

Rainer, Tristine. *The New Diary: How to Use a Journal for Self-Guidance and Expanded Creativity*, 2004, Penguin Group

Klauser, Henriette Anne. *Write It Down, Make It Happen: Knowing What You Want And Getting It*, 2000, Fireside Simon & Schuster Inc.

Neubauer, Joan. *Complete Idiot's Guide to Journaling*, 2001, Alpha Books, Macmillan

Little Picture Ritual—Task Timer

Task Timer: The Anti-Procrastination Timer by Endangered Apps.

itunes.apple.com/us/app/task-timer-the-anti-procrastination/id382035067?mt=8

My Top Celebration Music—Let's Dance!

1. Celebration – Kool and the Gang
2. What a Feeling (Flashdance) – Irene Cara
3. Walking on Sunshine – Katrina and the Waves
4. Dynamite – Taio Cruz
5. I Got a Feeling – Black Eyed Peas
6. I Just Want to Celebrate – Rare Earth
7. Sing a Song – Earth Wind and Fire
8. Don't Stop – Fleetwood Mac
9. You Ain't Seen Nothing Yet – BTO
10. Hold Your Head Up – Argent
11. Abracadabra – Steve Miller Band
12. Joy to the World – Three Dog Night
13. Taking Care of Business – BTO
14. I Like That Old Time Rock and Roll – Bob Seger
15. Let's Get It Started – Black Eyed Peas

Vision Boards

There are numerous online references available for helping you create a Vision Board. My favorite article is Martha Beck's article in the June 2010 issue of Oprah Magazine. www.oprah.com/spirit/How-to-Make-a-Vision-Board-Find-Your-Life-Ambition-Martha-Beck

Assaraf, John. *The Complete Vision Board Kit: Using the Power of Intention and Visualization to Achieve Your Dreams,* 2008. Atria Books, A Division of Simon & Schuster, Inc.

References

[1]Dent, David. "The A.D.D. Dilemma." www.inc.com/magazine/20050201/managing.html (February 1, 2005). Accessed 12/28/08.

[2]Young, Susan. "ADHD children grow up: An empirical review." *Counselling Psychology Quarterly* 13 (2000): 191–200. Accessed 12/28/08.

[3]Kopamees, Sara."Canada's Economic Edge. A Look Into 2010." *Canadian Business Journal,* www.cbj.ca/features/january_10_features/canada_s_economic_edge. html (2010). Accessed 12/28/08.

[4]Sabochik, Katelyn. "Small Businesses Are the Backbone of Our Economy and the Cornerstones of Our Communities." *The White House Blog* www.whitehouse.gov/blog/2010/08/17/small-businesses-are-backbone-our-economy-and-cornerstones-our-communities (2010). Accessed 12/28/08.

[5]Perel Essence Group. perelessencegroup.com/Target_Opportunities.htm. Accessed 12/28/08.

[6]Ranseen, Tom. "BADD: Business Attention Deficit Disorder." NoSpin Debunker #47 www.ranseenmarketing.com/online_marketing_library/ debunker/2002Debunkers/DebunkerJuly8_02.htm (July 8, 2002). Accessed 12/28/08.

[7]Giwerc, David. As quoted in Dent, David, *The ADD Dilemma.*

[8]Quily, Pete. "Top 10 Advantages of ADHD in a High Tech Career." adultaddstrengths.com/2006/02/09/top-10-advantages-of-add-in-a-high-tech-career/ (February 9, 2006). Accessed 05/05/10.

[9]World Health Organization, Adult Self-Report Scale-V1.1
(ASRS-V1.1)
www.gettingpaidtopayattention.com/adhd-test ASRS-v1-1.pdf

[10]Oxford Dictionary

[11]Steel, Piers. "The nature of procrastination: a meta-analytic
and theoretical review of quintessential self-regulatory failure."
Psychological Bulletin **131** (1)(2007): 65–94.
studiemetro.au.dk/fileadmin/www.studiemetro.au.dk/
Procrastination_2.pdf .
Accessed 07/07/11.

[12]Samalot, Diana. "How to Overcome Procrastination." *ArticlesBase*,
www.articlesbase.com/motivational-articles/how-to-overcome-
procrastination-1986368.html (March 14, 2010).
Accessed 07/07/10.

[13]Wikipedia, http://en.wikipedia.org/wiki/Procrastination.
Accessed 07/07/10.

[14]About Goal Setting. "Time Management Guide Part 16."
www.about-goal-setting.com/time-management-guide/16-
procrastination.html (Undated).
Accessed 07/07/11.

[15]Kahneman, D. "Maps of bounded rationality: Psychology for
behavioral economics." *American Economic Review, 93*(5) (2003):
1449–1475.

[16]Marano, Hara Estroff. "Procrastination: Ten Things to Know."
Psychology Today,
www.psychologytoday.com/articles/200308/procrastination-ten-
things-know (August 23, 2003).
Accessed 07/07/10.

[17]Jacobson, David. "The Danger in Delay, Combat Procrastination!"
WebMD Feature
www.webmd.com/balance/features/fight-procrastination (November
27, 2000).
Accessed 07/12/10.

[18]Ranseen, Tom. ibid

[19]Baldridge, Pat. "Mastering the art of effective meetings."As printed in *Winston-Salem Living* (November–December 2006). Accessed 12/28/08. Website not accessible May 27, 2010.

[20]Tergesen, Anne. "Feel Like You've Got ADD? Solutions for the Frazzled and Overwhelmed.*" Business Week,* www.businessweek.com/careers/workingparents/blog/ archives/2007/03/feel_like_youve_got_add_solutions_for_the_ frazzled_and_overwhelmed.html (March 1, 2007).

[21]Latino, Robert J. "The effects of distractions on human performance." Briefings on Patient Safety, *HCPro Patient Safety Monitor Journal* (June 2008).

[22]Safern, Judy. "New Business Book Diagnoses Corporate America with Attention Deficit Disorder." www.reuters.com/article/idUS109129+05-Feb-2008+PRN20080205 (February, 2008).

[23]Finn, Thom. "What is Entrepreneurial Attention Deficit Disorder?" (Undated). Found on www.actioncoach.com/What-is-Entrepreneurial-Attention-Deficit-Disorder?pressid=649. Accessed 07/12/11.

[24]Pressfield, Steven. *The War of Art: Break Through the Blocks and Win Your Inner Creative Battles.* Warner Books, 2002.

[25]Cirillo, Francesco. "The Pomodoro Technique (The Pomodoro)" downloaded as PDF from pomodorotechnique.com, 2006.

[26]Tracy, Brian. "ANTs v. CATs" *Brian Tracy International Blog,* www.briantracy.com/blog/blog-contest/jakibent (May 10, 2011). Accessed 08/12/11.

[27]Whipps, Heather. "Study Reveals Why We Get Distracted So Easily." *Live Science* www.livescience.com/7238-study-reveals-distracted-easily.html (March 29, 2007).

[28]Hallowell, Edward M. *Crazy Busy: Overstretched, Overbooked, and About to Snap! Strategies for Handling Your Fast-Paced Life.* Ballantine Books, 2007.

[29]Wikipedia, Continuous Partial Attention. Accessed 05/21/11.

[30]Giwerc, Dave. As quoted in Dent, David, "The ADD Dilemma".

[31]Lewis, Marilyn."The Upside of ADHD. Enthusiasm, empathy and high energy among traits the disorder carries." MSN Health. health.msn.com/health-topics/adhd/the-upside-of-adhd. (Undated). Accessed 12/7/11.

[32]Muehlhauser, Luke. "How to Beat Procrastination." lesswrong.com/lw/3w3/how_to_beat_procrastination/. (February 5, 2011). Accessed 08/12/11.

[33]Found in www.Searchquotes.com

[34]Marano, Hara Estroff. "Procrastination: Ten Things To Know." *Psychology Today* www.psychologytoday.com/articles/200308/procrastination-ten-things-know (August 23, 2003). Accessed 07/07/10.

[35]Habstritt, Greg. Simple Wealth, www.simplewealth.com/success-dna-detector. Accessed 08/11/11.

[36]Gilbert, Alorie. "Why can't you pay attention anymore?" CNET News, news.cnet.com/Why-cant-you-pay-attention-anymore---page-3/2008-1022_3-5637632-3.html?tag=mncol (March 28, 2005).

[37]Cirillo, Francesco. "The Pomodoro Technique (The Pomodoro)." 2006. Downloaded as PDF from pomodorotechnique.com 09/12/11.

[38]Singer, Blair. *The ABCs of Building a Business Team That Wins.* Warner Business Books, 2004.

[39]Hill, Napoleon. *Think and Grow Rich.* A Fawcett Crest Book, published by Ballantine Books, New York, Revised 1960: 169.

[40]Eker, T. Harv. Peak Potentials Training. www.peakpotentials.com.

[41]A special thank you to my BellyFit instructor, Tamara Logan of Kelowna from whom I first learned this self-High Five Technique. For more information on BellyFit please go to www.facebook.com/#!/pages/Tamara-Logan-Bellyfit-Yogini-Groover-Mover-Super-Hero/278280495548847.

About the Author

Marilyn Strong, a business and marketing strategist, is a solo entrepreneur who also has ADD/ADHD. Creative strategies help her get and stay focused, so she can enjoy following the shiny pennies then jump back into work or play. She lives in Kelowna, British Columbia with musician Scott Pembleton.

Made in the USA
Middletown, DE
26 August 2019